flying solo

Career Transition Tips for Singles

HALLIE CRAWFORD, MA, CPCC

Kick Ass Career Coaching Books • Atlanta

Published by Kick Ass Career Coaching Books, Atlanta, GA 30307
www.HallieCrawford.com
www.FlyingSoloBook.com

Cover and book design by Jill Anderson, www.JillLynnDesign.com

ISBN-13: 978-0-615-17557-7
ISBN-10: 0-615-17557-0

Library of Congress Control Number: 2008903246

Printed in the United States of America

1 3 5 7 9 10 8 6 4 2

Disclaimer: The information and recommendations in this book are presented in good faith and for general information purposes only. Every effort has been made to ensure the materials presented are accurate, that the information presented in the interviews was current and up to date at the time the interviews were conducted, and Web addresses were active at the time of printing. All information is supplied on the condition that the reader or any other person receiving the information will do their own due diligence and make their own determination as to its suitability for any purpose prior to any use of this information. The purpose of this material is to educate and entertain. The author, Hallie Crawford, and any affiliated companies shall have neither liability nor responsibility to any person or entity with respect to any loss or damage caused or alleged to have been caused, directly or indirectly, by the information contained in this book.

To my son, Vaughn Miller

Acknowledgments

I always wondered what I would write in this space when I finished my first book. Would it be the traditional thank you's, something witty or off the wall?

I decided to just go off the cuff: First, thank you for buying this book. I hope it gives you insight, motivation and much more. I want you to have a career you love and be able to make it happen just like I have.

A big thank you to my editors and writers, Veronica Yates, Stephanie Salter and Dina Giolitto. This would not be real without you. Huge appreciation for my coach Jeanna Gabbellini, who inspires me to be the best I can be as a coach, business owner and human being. To my client Tara Scarlett, who gave me the idea to write this book in the first place and provided invaluable feedback on the first draft—you are fab. There is a piece of each of you in this book and I thank you for being a part of it.

And a big thank you to my wonderful clients, who help make my job more rewarding and fulfilling than I could have ever imagined.

Finally, much love to my family, supportive loving hubby Frank, and our son Vaughn.

Hallie Crawford, MA, CPCC
Atlanta, GA

Table of Contents

flying solo

Career Transition Tips for Singles

Introduction

. . . .

The greatest risk in life is not taking one.

−ANONYMOUS

. . . .

When I was considering a career transition without the support of a spouse, the quote above kept me going. I would ask myself, "At the end of my life do I want to say I tried and failed, or that I hadn't tried at all?" You know the answer . . . I wanted to say that I tried. I wanted to say I stepped out of my comfort zone to take a stand for what I wanted in my life—a career I felt impassioned about, truly enjoyed, and one that would provide me with more than enough income to meet my financial goals. What do you want to say at the end of your life?

As an experienced career coach who started her career transition as a single gal, I am passionate about helping you make your career change smooth and successful. I know first hand that being single doesn't have to hold you back. In fact, as you go through this book you'll find your current single status can be an asset.

Singles I have coached tend to have a unique set of challenges when making a career transition, or when stepping into the workforce for the first time. No matter what your gender, age, or current experience, this book addresses those challenges specific to singles in today's marketplace. One of my clients, Tara Scarlett, underwent a dramatic career change. In talking with her about the difficulties, we found a lot of information out there for career seekers who have traditional support systems—a spouse or partner—but none specifically targeted to Singles. *Flying Solo: Career Transition Tips for Single*s answers that need. It provides practical tips you can use each day, methods you can apply at every crossroad during your transition.

But this book is not about singling out Singles and saying, "You have 'special' challenges so there's something wrong with you." Far from it. I am saying that I understand what you're going through and here's how you can overcome and manage any fears you face in the process. It's about managing transition. If you're still on the fence, you'll find quick tips in the very first chapter to help you determine when it's time to make the leap to your next career.

The Bottom Line: This book is about finding ways to remain financially stable, get the support you need, and triumph over your doubts and fears along the way. You can make it happen. There are many people who have successfully done this without a partner to support them financially or emotionally.

In Chapter Eight, I've included client success stories to inspire you toward your dreams. I thank them for allowing me to share their experiences with you as you go through this book creating your own success story.

I wish you the best in identifying your dream career and making it happen. And, if I can help you in any other way on your journey, feel free to get in touch!

Career-Minded Singles
Making a Change to Something Bigger and Better

. . . .

What would you do if you knew you could not fail?
—ANONYMOUS

. . . .

Welcome and congratulations on making the commitment to move toward a career that is bigger and better for you. Most likely you are either considering a career change, or have already begun laying the foundation for your next job. This could mean a new position, a new company, a new business of your own, or even a job in a brand new field.

Let's dive right in: Do you fall into the category of "I know I need to make a change and the time is now!" Or are you on the fence, still wondering if the place you are in is really a fit? Is it possible that you are unhappy for some other reason than the job? Whether you're single or not, being uncertain about making a change is *completely normal*. Having doubts and fears is common.

Career change can be a very big deal; work is a major part of our lives. We spend a lot of time there and our jobs pay the bills. Plus, making a career transition takes time, effort, and a certain amount of risk. It's understandable that you want to make sure you are investing your time and money wisely.

For those who are 100% certain the time to make a change is now, feel free to skip this section. But if you're on the fence, feeling wobbly about whether a job change is the right thing to do, or if it's the best time to tackle career transition, read on. The "Red Flag Test" will give you some questions to consider that will help you come to a decision.

THE RED FLAG TEST
How To Know When It's Time To Go

We all have our ups and downs at work so it's important to define whether you really need to change jobs, or if you're just going through a rough patch you need to work through. For me, I knew it was time to go when I found myself crying in the bathroom at work. Yes, this is a little embarrassing to admit, but it's true. And I've spoken to many people who have done the same thing. That same day I even tried the "girlie" method of feeling better—retail therapy—to see if buying a new suit would boost my feelings about my job. It didn't work.

Red Flags—Signs That It's Time to Make a Change

↪ **You dread getting out of bed in the morning—every morning.** Do you repeatedly hit the snooze button? Do you have an *overwhelming* desire to stay buried under the covers, far from demands, deadlines, and clamoring co-workers? One of the biggest red flags of job dissatisfaction is an unwillingness to face the day—not just some mornings, but every morning. What's your body trying to tell you?

↪ **Your work relationships and performance are beginning to suffer.** You start to avoid certain people and tasks and you're not doing your job as well as you used to. Remember when group projects were productive and enjoyable, chatting with co-workers in the hall was a pleasant break from the daily routine and "Happy Hour" truly was happy? If you now find yourself avoiding particular persons and duties, slacking on your reviews or *really* dreading company outings, chances are you've lost that loving feeling for your job.

↪ **You work tirelessly,** even staying late to accomplish tasks or finish projects because you feel like you have to, but you get no joy or satisfaction from what you produce for your company anymore.

↪ **You start to slack off at work and have little or no motivation to perform.** And this isn't just a few days a month; it's become a regular occurrence. You spend a good part of your workdays immersed in "escapist" activities—nonessential e-mailing, surfing the Internet, or micro-managing a project in order to procrastinate. You find yourself playing the avoidance game in any way you can. This is definitely a sign that something is wrong.

☞ **You become "someone else" at work.** If you feel like you can't be yourself at work, don't shrug it off and don't blame yourself. Every company's culture is different. Yours may not be aligned, or no longer aligned, with who you are *now* as a person. Know that there are professional people out there who embrace the same goals and values as you do. Maybe it's time to stop pretending, to stop being someone other than who you are, and seek out those like-minded professionals.

☞ **The position doesn't make use of your talents.** Perhaps you're an advertising executive who always wanted to be a chef. Perhaps your job title is "coordinator," but you feel much more the creative type. If your job is not utilizing your natural talents and abilities, it's probably not a fit for you.

☞ **You spend most of your time complaining about your job.** Sure, we all tend to commiserate over frustrating aspects of our jobs, and other things in our lives for that matter. But if most of your hours at work are spent feeding on negative thoughts and verbally expressing them, this is a huge red flag. It may be time to pack it in.

꘡꘡ **Finally, if you regularly fantasize about quitting your job, being fired or let go,** this is a sure sign your current position is not a fit for you—time to move on!

If any of these red flags are waving at you, it's probably time to seriously consider changing jobs, whether it's moving into a new position at your current company or changing your course completely by choosing an entirely different career path. Whatever you do, don't remain miserable.

• • • • •

Now that you are clear about whether it is time to move forward with your career transition, you are in a stronger position to do something about it. These days most people want more than a paycheck; they want to be happy and fulfilled in their jobs. More and more people are doing something about it, and now so are you!

Times Have Changed: No Waiting on Fulfillment

Our parents may have just bucked up and taken the ups and downs of their jobs without giving a thought to changing careers. They stayed where they were, collected their pensions and retired. Only then did they begin to really enjoy their lives. Times are different now. People want satisfying, rewarding careers. They're no longer content to just punch a time clock. They want a sense of fulfillment from their work and they expect to enjoy their lives *now* instead of waiting until retirement.

The good news is this: now we can and are doing it. Vast numbers of career-minded singles have already done it, and increasing numbers are in the process of achieving greater fulfillment every day.

People also change jobs more frequently than ever before, and they demand more perks and benefits from their jobs. They're not willing to settle for less than a job they truly enjoy, nor are they inclined to follow in the footsteps of their parents or previous generations in a job market that has changed dramatically.

The facts: Today it's not unusual for people to have as many as five-to-seven different jobs in a lifetime. With the explosion of the Internet and telecommuting, more people can work from home, start their own businesses, or work part-time on their own terms. Work hours are more flexible and employees have become more demanding. They want, and are demanding, more free time, flex time to work, and greater benefit packages than offered in the past.

People are also staying single longer. There are millions of people out there just like you who want more from their work lives and are going through the same challenges to find their ideal careers. So know that you are not alone. [1]According to the US Census Bureau's 2004 survey, 49.8 percent of the nation's 109.9 million housing units list the

. . . .

[1] United States Census Bureau: The 2007 Statistical Abstract, The National Data Book. Accessed at http://www.census.gov/compendia/statab/ on August 12, 2007

head of household as unmarried. That is up from 48.3 percent by the full census in 2000. Some 29.6 million people in the United States live alone. The Bureau of Labor Statistics estimates that about 42 percent of the entire workforce is unmarried, just under half of the total workforce—that's a lot of single people.

Starting Out Right: Identify Obstacles, Get the Support You Need

No matter what career transition stage you're in, admitting that you need extra help is an important stride forward. I can't stress enough the value of getting support during your transition. It is difficult to do it all yourself, and you don't have to. Support is all around you and the answers are within easy reach. We'll discuss specific singles support resources throughout the book, but for now know that you have all the inner strength that's needed to move on with a plan no matter where you are in the process.

While changing jobs can be difficult for everyone, as a single person you have a unique set of challenges that may feel completely different from those who are not flying solo. I know that being single can feel great on some days and not so great on others. Some days you probably feel completely carefree and unencumbered, able to go anywhere and do anything you want to because you have no personal obligations or responsibilities to anyone else. You could pick up and travel the world if you really wanted to.

On other days, you don't feel so excited about being single. You feel more alone than anything else. You may question where your life is going and you might start comparing yourself to your attached friends, wondering if and when you'll be on that path. Or if you even want to be. On these days it can feel like something is missing.

So what do you do on the days when "blissfully unencumbered" suddenly makes you feel sorry for yourself, more like a victim of circumstance? We will address feelings of loneliness, aloneness or "feeling lost" throughout this book, but it is important to remember that being single during a career transition has many advantages.

When you're single, you have the freedom to make your own decisions and to take greater risks and you'll be joining millions of singles who are in the midst of making successful career transitions for themselves every day. You can do it too.

You may feel as though you have only yourself to rely on for financial, mental, and emotional support. This is understandable, but it doesn't have to be that way. The chapters ahead will help you change those feelings with methods for identifying and garnering sources of support while you learn to overcome any obstacles that stand in the way of your career transition.

By the end of this book, you will learn to:

- Identify obstacles that stand between you and a rewarding, successful career.
- Find solutions and "workarounds" to those obstacles.

- Define your support system and find the people who can help you get where you need to be.
- Carve out a transition plan that will help you forge ahead.
- Jumpstart your networking skills.
- Excel at developing a Killer Resume for any position.
- Perform confidently at every interview (See Bonus Sections).

Career Transition Challenges

Single or otherwise, everyone faces challenges when making a career transition. I work with people every day who are moving through career transition challenges with greater ease than they thought possible. At first, change itself can be uncomfortable and this is a completely normal feeling. Finding a new job is usually not on our top ten list of fun things to do! It takes an investment in time and money, and it requires a certain amount of risk-taking to jump into the next best thing.

As a single person flying solo, be prepared to address specific challenges as well as more general issues that you may encounter while undergoing your professional transformation. Know that *all* of these challenges can be overcome with some thought and commitment on your part. And here's a tip: if you consistently work toward remaining positive and focused as much as possible, it's going to be much easier than you think.

Notice I didn't say remain positive and focused 100% of the time. This is certainly something to strive for, and you're going to have down days when you don't feel great about your transition. We all do. Give yourself permission to have both good and bad days. Be kind to yourself. We'll discuss this further in Chapter 5.

Challenge 1: Financial Stability During Transition

In many ways, our emotional and mental health is tied to our financial well-being. Does this ring true for you? The need to remain financially stable so you can pay your bills and maintain your lifestyle is vitally important to everyone. And, it can be a challenge that singles feel more acutely than those who have someone to lean on financially. Depending on an individual's financial situation, this is a considerable challenge for both men and women.

During a career transition, you may have to cut back in some places where you're used to spending and, instead, invest time, money, and energy in other areas you may not feel comfortable with just yet. We'll discuss these areas in detail later on. This cutting back may not sound like fun at first (it didn't to me!) and it may feel unfamiliar. Just trust that any sacrifices you make to have a career you love are going to be well worth it in the end. I'm speaking not only from my own experience, but from my experience with clients who have succeeded in their career transitions using the same tips and methods you'll be applying to your own.

To help you remain financially stable during your transition, start by making small sacrifices one at a time. This way you'll become more comfortable with financial adjustments over time. I don't recommend slashing your spending drastically, doing so could cause a sense of deprivation which will make you unhappy. Too many large cuts too fast will not help. Your energy level and attitude are going to suffer, and you'll have more trouble remaining positive and focused. Instead, start small and choose sacrifices you can live with, knowing you don't have to give these things up permanently. More on this in Chapter Four.

Commit to something small, like eating at home every night during the week to save money you might otherwise spend dining out. And while you're doing this, keep in mind that you are not giving this up forever. You will be able to eat out as often as you like once you've made your transition.

Believe me, once you get a better handle on your finances the rest will fall into place more easily. Even the smallest sacrifice, such as the example of eating at home more, empowers you because you can measure the results right away in the money you save—savings you can put toward your transition.

You can and will get through it.

Challenge 2: Emotional and Mental Focus

Maintaining a positive attitude, remaining focused and motivated, and managing your emotions are all very important aspects in making your career transition successful. I will touch on this subject frequently throughout the book. The more you learn to motivate yourself and manage your energy level and attitude, the better. Attending to your emotional and mental needs will help keep you stable during this change and it will better enable you to overcome any obstacles that get in your way. Without doing this, you could end up slowing down your progress or worse—giving up and staying put in your current job because you choose not to face the challenges of making a change. But that's not what you want. Taking good care of yourself mentally and emotionally will keep you focused on what you seek: a fulfilling new career.

Again, this doesn't mean you're going to feel great every step of the way during your transition. Everyone gets emotional, frustrated or unmotivated from time to time. It's understandable and normal. The key is to learn what to do when you hit that wall so you can take steps to overcome those blocks.

Stop and take a few minutes to reflect on why you started this process in the first place. What is it you wanted to achieve? Reflecting on your strongest initial motivation reconnects you with your goal and reminds you why it was and is exciting to you. This will help you get out of the rut and motivated again.

You can prepare yourself for the potential ups and downs by deciding what activities or commitments you are going to put into place to maintain your mental health and happiness. Just make sure you are doing things you truly enjoy *on a regular basis.*

Here are a couple of examples:

- **Make a commitment to maintain your exercise routine.** It will boost your energy and mental state.
- **Start a list of things you enjoy that make you happy** and commit to doing something on that list once a week, like going to the movies, hanging out with friends, or taking your dog for a walk.

Finally, as a single, sometimes it can take a bit longer to work your way out of those down cycles. Why? Simply because singles don't always reach out and ask for support when they need it most. Before you embark on your transition, think about who you'll use for support. You can choose a friend, family member, a professional career coach or even better, a combination of all three. Reach out to them *ahead of time* and ask for their support. You're *preparing* for transition. And, by letting them know in advance, you're preparing them as well. Remember to keep reaching out to these same people throughout your transition. You'll be glad you did.

We'll discuss the topic of support all along the way. By the end of this book, you will know how to build and maintain a support system that will help keep your mental and emotional health in balance.

Challenge 3: Feeling Stuck and Getting Unstuck

Another common problem for singles (and many career seekers for that matter) is feeling stuck. You're caught between the old job that you know and trust and the promise of a new career where you could be doing something much better. Even though you may be unhappy, your current job can feel like a comfortable t-shirt or pair of shoes. In your current job you know what to expect; there are no surprises; it's familiar territory and that's comfortable. You're stuck.

Or maybe you feel lost and unsure of what to do next. You want to move ahead, but you don't know what to do or where to start. Maybe you do know what to do next, but you're not sure in what order to do it or how to get yourself motivated. Again, you're stuck.

Just like getting stuck happened for you one step at time, getting unstuck happens in the same way. Even the smallest forward movement will make a big difference. Take it step-by-step.

I've come across many career seekers who want to know everything they need to do in order to make a career transition. And, they want to know the entire process before they take any action. This is *not* what I mean by taking things step-by-step.

If you feel the need to know all the steps before you take one, my advice is this: Just get started. There is no "one way" or one process to make career change successful for everyone. Each person's plan of action will look different. It depends on your situation, your goals, and how drastic a change you want to make.

Don't over-think what you're doing here to the point you become frozen and find yourself unable to take any action. You can plan for your career transition to a certain extent but you can't plan everything, nor can you predict the future. Just get started—know that the plan will unfold as you move forward. Commit yourself to seeing this as an adventure and to trusting your judgment along the way. You will figure this out just like you've figured out other dilemmas in your life.

Here's good news: The sooner you take even the smallest step forward, the closer you'll be to your new career and something bigger and better. One step at a time.

It has often been said that the number one reason most people don't start what they want to start, is because they think their simple, small efforts won't even dent the mountain they wish to move. But that's exactly how the mountain was formed!

Challenge 4: Single But Married to the Job

Ever feel like you're married to your job? Join the club. Single people are often highly dedicated to their jobs. You are far from alone. And in general, singles tend to be more invested in their careers than their married coworkers. Employers sometimes view singles this way as well, however biased a viewpoint that may be. Your next job interview is the time to address and clarify your boundaries. Since employers may tend to view singles differently, you need to define your boundaries early so you can ward off any possible assumptions that you'll be more willing to give everything to your job. Employers often take for granted that you'll give all your energy and time, and extra time (if you have any left) to working harder and longer.

To be fair, there are reasons this bias exists. Take a look around your workplace. Who are you more likely to see taking on extra responsibilities? Who stays after hours to get work done, and who is generally more consumed with what's happening on the job? Singles like yourself, right? Of course, there are always exceptions. But for many singles the job becomes the top priority and everything else falls in step behind.

If you're practically married to your job, as much as you may dream of leaving, you're probably attached to the job on some level or it may be a large factor in defining who you are in the world. These are totally normal feelings for a single, but they can hold you back from making the changes you want to make. It may be time to consider divorcing your job, or at least look into "separating" and getting some guidance so that you are in a better position to move ahead in your career transition.

Here's the deeper issue:

Our jobs often help define us not only for ourselves, but also for others. How many times have you been introduced to someone new and the first thing they say after "Hello" is "What do you do?" This can be especially true for men, who are more frequently defined by their professions. Also, work is a place where we spend the greater part of our time; it often provides our primary social network. Therefore, leaving something behind that is such a large part of who we are can be difficult for anyone, and especially challenging for singles.

Many factors come into play as we consider making the move to something bigger and better for ourselves. Our desire to make a difference often tops the list—it really matters to us.

We've likely thrown our "whole selves" into doing the best we can at our jobs, which, in terms of career development, is usually a good thing. It does, however, make it awfully difficult to say goodbye when the time comes to move forward in our careers. And that's a pretty good reason to feel stuck. You want to make a move, yet you're immobilized by what saying goodbye means. You'll likely wonder not only how it will affect your paycheck, but your social network and sense of identity as well.

Finally, the old job feels familiar and comfortable—too comfortable. Feeling comfy in your current job can sometimes seem like a good enough reason to stay put even when you're unhappy. The job may fit you like an old, comfy pair of slippers, but that doesn't mean you don't need new slippers. Sure, your job has let you down at times, but at least you know what to expect, right? Along with the familiarity of the work itself, some coworkers have become an extended family. It's tough to break free from all that and veer off into a new and possibly scary direction.

The Good and Better News

People at your new job will soon need your skills, talents, insights and know-how just as much as those at your current job. New things do become familiar in time. Pretty soon you'll have room for a new routine, new faces, places, and a new and exciting set of opportunities and learning experiences.

Even if you're doubtful, feeling unsure or lost, know that you are not alone and such feelings are to be expected. The tips in this book will help you work out the kinks. You're going to make it happen for yourself—one step at a time.

Of course, it *will* take commitment and diligence to overcome some of the challenges, but believe me when I say that the payoffs and benefits are worth it. Years from now you will look at this period as time well spent and the investment you made worth every penny.

You Have More Control Than You Might Think

If you're like other singles who throw themselves into their jobs, your career has probably been the basis for many life decisions. Consider where you live or the plans you may be making for your future home. You typically make those types of plans according to whatever location your job dictates, right?

Now consider what would happen if, say, your company decided to downsize and to leave you behind. Suddenly you find yourself living in a city that you may not have lived in had it been up to you in the first place, leading a life that's been dictated primarily by your job. This is what happens to people who let their careers dictate their lives. But it doesn't have to happen to you.

As many career seekers learn, one of the most liberating feelings you can experience is a sense of control over your own life. That means, instead of taking your cue from the company you work for, learning when to say, "No thanks, that's not the direction I'd like to head." It's about finding the strength to pick up and go your own way, despite fear of the unknown.

• • • • •

Time for another check in: What type of Career Seeker are you? Do you already know what your dream job is or are you still uncertain? If you are still uncertain, take some time to figure this out or contact me for some coaching. It's crucial to know where you're headed.

Although this book is not specifically, nor only, about helping you define your dream, I've included some tips to help you begin to clarify your dream. Let's discuss this for a moment. Before you make a career transition, you need to know not only where you're going, but what type of career seeker you are. In the next section, under Career Seeker Type B, I'll give you some tips to help you get started on identifying your passion—one of the initial steps toward clarifying your dream.

Types of Career Seekers

Just because you know you're ready for a career change doesn't mean you know what you'd like to do—or does it?

For some career seekers, the path is very clear. They know what they want, what's important to them and they are ready to make it happen. But for others, conflicting talents and interests can cloud the decision-making process. This is normal. Many people have so many diverse interests that they can't decide which one to pursue. This can make the process confusing.

So, before you get started on your career change, explore the two Career Seeker Type profiles to determine which one fits your *current* situation or state of mind.

Career Seeker Type A: I Know My Dream

You are this type if you have:

- **An exact mental picture of what you'd like to be doing in your next career.** You just need to get started.
- **An idea of what you want to be doing.** You just need to clarify that idea by doing some research, determining your options for making it happen, and developing your plan of action.
- **A clear sense of your passion.** You just need to figure out how to turn it into a lucrative career path.

As Career Seeker Type A, maybe you see yourself owning your own company, opening up a shop, or starting a business online. Perhaps you've always wanted to work in a particular field in which you excel, such as technology, web design, writing, crafts, mathematics, science, child psychology, or wherever your interests and talents lie. Possibly you have a specific skill that you've developed over the years and you now feel ready to turn that gift into a lucrative career.

For you, there should be less of a need for self-exploration. You already know your capabilities, interests and passion. More emphasis will be needed on what's required to get there. More than anything else, you will need to set your personal goals and develop a practical plan that you will commit to and carry out step-by-step from start to finish.

You've already taken the first step: you've decided to make a career change. Next, you'll develop empowering behaviors and habits that will keep you on the path to successfully making the change. You'll learn how to prevent yourself from lapsing into any old, self-defeating behaviors that have held you back from achieving your goals in the past.

As a single person with an abundance of personal freedom, you are ready to focus most on staying true to the goals you've now set in motion—no matter how your feelings and moods fluctuate from day to day, and no matter who or what throws a temporary monkey wrench in your plans. As you forge ahead into uncharted and exciting territory, you'll find new ways to stay on track and maintain your motivation.

Remember, the challenges and obstacles you face can be overcome with persistence, focus, and drive.

Career Seeker Type B: Still Looking for the Dream

You are this career seeker if you:

- **Have several different ideas** for possible career choices and aren't yet sure which one to pick.
- **Feel lost, or have no idea** what it is you'd like to do and need help figuring it out.

If you resonate with the Career Seeker Type B, don't despair. It's perfectly okay to feel unsure about where you're headed professionally. Simply put: You can and will figure this out; millions of people have.

Still uncertain? Quite often, people who say they don't know what their dream is, actually *do* have one; they just aren't consciously aware of it. Your dreams may have become buried under years of doubts, fears, or believing that they can't happen, so much so that to you it may seem the dream has disappeared.

Take a moment to consider this: As a child, what did you dream about doing when you grew up? Did you have a vision or a desire to be a photographer, actor, astronaut or something else? Know that this dream is still there inside of you, and there may be something to it.

Is there a childhood dream that has been buried and just needs to be uncovered?

You can now take time to dream anew. You may be pleasantly surprised at the career connections you now can make as an adult with those childhood dreams as the springboard. New possibilities are likely to emerge.

Sometimes Type B Seekers worry they'll find themselves drifting from job to job in the midst of career confusion. Look instead at this concern from the positive side. When you're single, there truly is no better time in your life to be trying on different career roles. Yes, you have legitimate concerns about remaining financially stable and keeping a roof over your head. Even so, when you're flying solo there's so little weighing you down. Many singles before you have found creative ways to support themselves during a career change. You can too.

What is your specific area of expertise? Could you freelance on the side? Sell yourself as a consultant? Perhaps you can do temp or contract work on weekends. There are numerous sales rep possibilities as well. Are there products you like and use regularly? Do these companies offer ways you can sign up as a rep and develop a second stream of income? If so, you'd be promoting something you're already sold on yourself, which would make selling easy for you.

Use this time in your life to really get to know yourself and to discover your untapped talents. You'll be well on your way to narrowing down your ideas and career options to the very best of them.

The Benefits of Following Your Dream

As you allow yourself to pursue your dream, you will discover you have the confidence, smarts, and willpower to get where you want to be. Any hesitation and worry you may be experiencing now will be replaced with newfound confidence and a sense of personal accomplishment. Even in the early transition stage, you may be surprised to find a sense of greater fulfillment at work and home simply because you have begun moving forward in a more powerful, positive direction.

When you begin acting on your career dream, you'll also start to feel a sense of *purpose*. You feel inspired and it feels good. This is how it works!

Think about this: when you feel frustrated about something at work, you probably bring those concerns home, even though you try your best to prevent it from happening. This is understandable because every area of our lives affects the other areas. We're human. So the opposite will occur as you move closer to achieving your dream. You will naturally bring that sense of anticipation of fulfillment to areas outside of your career.

It gets better. Once you have experienced this greater sense of fulfillment at work, you will be inspired to make changes in other areas to match the satisfaction you have created in your career. It's the "all boats rise with the tide" idea. You won't want to settle for less in your relationships or any other area of your personal life. That's a good thing. It will keep you motivated to strive for even more.

2

Getting Your Transition Started
Dream First, Dream Big

You know the traditional image of the American Dream: Work hard and you can have anything you want, regardless of where you came from, your socio-economic status or any other aspect of your life. Everyone can have the traditional American Dream. Well, the American Dream has changed, and the traditional way to pursue that dream is quite different. No longer is there just one "work hard" ethic to achieve the American Dream. And, it's no longer about sticking to one career path for the rest of your life.

More and more people are entrepreneurs, or well on the way to becoming them. They're starting their own businesses—some very non-traditional ones. Think of online dating websites, the boom in the consulting industry, and small business owners like myself. Market and consumer trends have changed significantly, and some would say radically. It all adds up to this: Today the world really is your oyster. There are so many ways to make money and earn a living. The idea of having multiple streams of income is not unusual; it is starting to become the norm. But, you can't expect your dream job to unfold in front of you like a 1950s-era corporate ladder.[2] You need to go after the dream job and create what you want. And you get to create your career from scratch, not from a cookie cutter or a corporate mold. As a single person you have even more freedom to set up your career, to break the mold, and figure out what will work for you. The process of "Dreaming First" will help you stay outside the box and think creatively about your career transition.

Tap into those secret fantasies about the ideal career for you and then use those insights into yourself to create a workable plan for the future. You've got nothing to lose, other than a missed opportunity because you waited too long. Today you're single, you're free, and the future is wide open. So take off your practical hat, put on your dreaming glasses and dream BIG.

· ·

[2] The Brazen Careerist Blog by Penelope Trunk, http://blog.penelopetrunk.com/

How 'Dreaming First' Works for You

I introduce my career coaching clients to the concept of "Dreaming First" early in our relationship. This is the initiation into their career change *before* they start making a plan for their career transitions.

When it's actually time to lay the groundwork for achieving a goal, we usually start with a plan for making it happen that includes practical steps along the way, but things invariably work out even better when they begin with a vision of exactly how they want things to progress before going on to the more concrete practical side.

So, let's start with *your dream first.*

Why dream first? Why turn to the fanciful side of your brain when everyone keeps telling you that a practical plan is the key to success? Because it works.

While a practical plan is one of the strongest keys to success, the best-laid plans always start with the dream—a dream that you can trim and shape later to fit your real-life situation.

One way to dream BIG is to use the technique of visualization. Successful people have used this technique for a very long time. Professional athletes do it; opera singers do it; and just about anyone seriously looking to enhance performance does it. Australian psychologist Alan Richardson performed an experiment published in *Research Quarterly*[3] which found that athletes who visualized every day for 20

[3] Sports Visualizations by Keith Randolph, http://www.llewellynencyclopedia. com/article/244

days, enhanced their performance by 23 percent. Richardson reported that the most effective visualization occurs when the visualizer both feels and sees what he is doing.

You can do the same thing: envision how you want your career transition to unfold, visualize the pieces you want to have in place to make it happen and "see" all the players you need to support you along the way. When you develop your vision first, you will not only become clearer about what you want to happen, you will also be more likely to make it happen in the way you've envisioned it, and therefore be successful.

Dreaming First is especially important because jumping into the practical side of your career transition too soon can squash your creative thinking. For example, say your ideal career path is to be an entrepreneur and own a restaurant. If you start doing research about owning your own café, you may get discouraged by the numbers of restaurants that never get off the ground or fail in the first several years. You may feel daunted before you've even gotten started. When you are in this dreaming phase, keep the negative voices at bay. Push them aside in this stage because they will only hold you back. In the planning and implementing phase of your transition you will need to learn how to actively manage them, and listen to them if they have some wisdom to share. But just for now, push these voices aside entirely.

If you dream first and allow yourself to think out of the box, you may start to imagine multiple ways you could succeed, for instance, in the example of starting your own restaurant. You could find a partner who's experienced in the business, look into purchasing a franchise, or come up with some other option you'd never have thought of had you not taken the time to dream first.

Dreaming First enables you to brainstorm as many possibilities as you can imagine for living out your dream, and therefore, enables you to identify many more ways to make it happen. If you start with practical planning first, you may get caught in "there's only one way to do this," when in actuality there may be several other ways that would work out perfectly for your situation. Dreaming First helps you discover them. So allow your mind to wander, be open to possibility and hold off on practical planning for the moment. We'll get to it in the next chapter.

Dream Journaling and Visualization

Two great tools for Dreaming First are journaling and visualization. You get to choose. Depending on whether you are a visual person or not, one of these tools may work better than the other for you. But try them both, you may find using a combination of the two is the most effective. Both tools will help you become more focused on how you want your career transition to unfold, and will make what you want to happen much more likely.

Whether you're dream journaling or visualizing, write down the results of your process—how you dreamed your ideal situation unfolded, how things went for you at a job interview or at a networking event. Did you imagine yourself as confident and articulate at the interview or being at the top of your game? Remember, if you can see it in your mind's eye, you can make it happen.

You can also dream the ideal end result of a situation, like imagining how you feel in your new career, picturing what your ideal day is like. What are you doing? Who is involved? Include anything you want in your dream and do it in a way that works for you.

Remember to write and dream *as if it has already happened*. Good luck!

Your Quick Start Tips on 'Dreaming First'

✓ Start with a blank slate in your mind.

✓ Always act from the present and what you really want, not from past experience. While you are creating your dream as if it has already happened, recognize that this is new—your chance to make your life and career exactly as you want it to be. Take advantage of it.

✓ Commit to making your choices as independently as possible from the voices of your past—your parents, the media, past experience, previous failures or successes, and assumptions. In this early phase of Dreaming First, I suggest not sharing your dream with others unless you are sure they will be supportive and provide encouragement. It helps to solidify your dream in your own mind before sharing it.

✓ Throw away any preconceived notions you have about transition being hard, about not being able to have a job you love or whatever assumptions you have that hold you back.

✓ Jump into the realm of possibility. Think and act only from there. I often tell my clients to make decisions from a place or perspective of possibility, not fear or lack. Decisions made out of fear almost never go right. The question is "Are you going to design your future, or is your past going to keep doing it for you?" (excerpt from *The Pathfinder*, p. 191) You get to decide.

✓ As you conjure up your dream scenario for your career transition, ask, "What's the best thing that could happen for me?" Ask this question each step of the way and write down your answers.

Dream Journaling Guidelines

Dream journaling involves writing out the process of your career transition in an ideal light, *as if it has already happened*. I suggest you use a Career Journal, a specific notebook dedicated to your transition. In it you'll create your dreams, list your "real life" actions, and be able to track your progress efficiently.

Your goal here is to include as many details in your Career Journal as possible with as much energy and excitement as you can *as if it has already happened*. Part of this process is about getting you pumped up to tackle your transition with heightened positive energy.

Here are some other things to dream about that will help make your journaling process easy and successful.

Include in your dream journaling:

1. The timeframe in which you achieved your goal— six months, one year?
2. How did you feel during this transition? Confident, clear, focused?
3. Make a list of those personal characteristics you tapped into and any new qualities you identified.
4. Where did you need extra support and where did you get it from?

Dreaming Visualization Guidelines

1. **First, take a deep breath.** Right now, take in a long, deep breath. Release any pressure or tension you might be feeling as you exhale fully. When you are tense and tight, nothing flows. Your thoughts tend to be restrictive, limited and self-defeating. Breathe deeply and easily. Allow yourself to let your dreaming flow. New possibilities will emerge.

2. **Include anything you want.** Visualize things that came up for you in the journaling exercise. The difference here is simply that you are imagining it in your mind instead of writing it down on paper.

3. **Have fun with it.** Be creative and dream BIG.

4. **If you find yourself starting to doubt what you're seeing or feeling, just let that image go.** Return to a visual that feels better, or create a new one. There's no room for doubt here, this is about dreaming. Remember, you'll work out "the how" later when it's time to get practical. For now, focus on the ideal.

5. **Create a structure for your vision.** A structure will constantly remind you of your vision and help keep you on track. Your structure can be anything you want it to be: a drawing, painting, images that you cut out of a magazine, a word or a quote that reminds you of your vision. Do what feels best for you and makes the most sense.

6. **Imagine your transition complete.** Relax and enjoy the feeling that it has unfolded perfectly for you.

When You've Completed Your Dream

Now come back to the real world and take a few minutes to think about what happened. How did it go? How did you act? Answer these questions in your Career Journal.

Next, take time to jot down areas in which you tend to stumble or have trouble in real life. Use the list of Blocks to Success on the next page to identify where you will need to be extra committed, and where you may need to ask for support from an external source, such as a friend, mentor, or a coach.

Identifying Blocks to Success

. . . .

Rate the following on a scale of 1-7 in terms of how much you struggle with each of them. 7 = struggle constantly with this block; 1 = never struggle in this area:

_____ Fear of failure   _____ Organizational skills

_____ Fear of success   _____ Self-confidence

_____ Procrastination   _____ Limiting beliefs

_____ Perfectionism   _____ Negative thinking

_____ Time management   _____ Self-discipline

_____ Assertiveness   _____ Goal setting

Resistance to   Stagnation in
_____ asking for help   _____ comfort zones

In any area where you rated yourself at a 6 or higher, decide how you will begin to work on overcoming this block during your career transition. Determine how you will handle each block by making a commitment to take action to overcome it, and be sure to ask for the support you need in doing so. For example, if you struggle with organizational skills, your commitment could be to create a folder on your computer dedicated to your career search documents. Or you could create a special email address and inbox to use solely for your career transition correspondence.

Keep On Dreaming First

Dreaming First will continue to be an important part of your career transition. The more you use the Dream First process, the more fine-tuned your dreams become. Throughout the ongoing transition process, consider how you want things to progress in each of these specific areas of your life: financial, emotional, mental, and physical.[4] What is your goal in each of these areas? Write them down in your Career Journal. Again, remember that you are writing and refining your dream *as if it has already happened.*

For example, in the financial area, you might write, "I had plenty of money to meet all of my needs during my career transition." And if you have a specific monthly budget in mind or an amount you need to live on for several months, include that amount of money.

For the emotional area, you could say, "I had all the emotional support and encouragement I needed from friends and family. They supported me every step of the way when I experienced doubts or fears about making my career transition happen."

[4] *I Can't Believe I Get Paid To Do This!* by Stacey Mayo

Then add anything else you want. Maybe you were the guest of honor at a party celebrating your success. Or perhaps you were so successful you were able to give a party for others you'd helped succeed. Maybe you're headed for the airport on your way to Italy for a three-week vacation where you'll meet a friend at a villa in Tuscany. Write it all down in your Career Journal. Have fun with it.

3

Setting Goals & Getting Practical
Your Personal Transition Plan

Now that you have identified your dream transition, it's time to jump into your practical plan. One of the most challenging aspects of making a career change is learning how to harness your passion and dreams and how to make them happen by creating a personal, practical transition plan. It's time to bring your perfect career fantasy to life and turn it into a workable plan that you can knock out step-by-step.

Step 1: Make the Commitment

Any big change you want to make in your life requires commitment and perseverance. It all starts with commitment. Think about how committed you are to making your career change. Are you truly dedicated to expanding your professional horizons?

If you are the type who has trouble sticking to something and seeing it through to completion, acknowledge this, and then commit to working on your new career transition 100%. Being single gives you an enormous advantage—no distractions from others, no excuses for not seeing it through. Your career transition is actually the best reason you have to do things differently; it's a brand new beginning.

Commit To Yourself First. If you are at the other end of the spectrum, a person married to your job, then committing to your career transition poses a different challenge. You will need to work on learning to shift the focus from your current job back to yourself. Instead of giving 110% every day at work, it's time to take back what's yours— your future. Give yourself permission each day to set aside time to work toward your own new career goals instead of always working for someone else. Tell yourself: *I'm going to make room in my life for a new commitment*—the promise to do something great for myself and my career.

Commit To the Change. We all have experience in making and keeping commitments. Some commitments like raising children are lifelong. Others, like deciding what to have for lunch, are strictly in the here-and-now. Being committed to a career change falls in the middle. It's something that you can feasibly do, at least for a while. And, if at some point, you want to "do it over again," you can develop a new plan and a new set of commitments. You can be flexible. But don't wait until retirement to follow your passion. Do it now.

A career change can be one of life's biggest and most rewarding transitions. Although it requires dedication, patience and persistence, people who successfully achieve their goals find ways to motivate themselves and stay motivated. They overcome obstacles and remain focused and determined throughout the process. But as a single, you know that this can be a lonely place. Take heart, no one is an island. Millions of other people out there are going through the same things you are, single and otherwise. You'll find ways to seek them out. Chapter Six and the Networking for Singles section will help you with this.

For right now, you can think about how you manage to stay motivated and committed in other areas of your life — social activities, staying fit, eating right, keeping a pet, having friends, and managing your finances. Can you apply the same strategy or philosophy to your career? What action, large or small, can you take today to move up the commitment scale? Write it down in your Career Journal. It could be anything from doing a bit of research to making a phone call.

Commitment Exercise

Ask the important questions—and be honest with yourself. If you're not ready to commit, it's better to admit it and then work on the things you need to take care of first, rather than dive in before you're really ready to make a change.

Getting Clear on Your Level of Commitment

Before you undertake a transition or take a step in your personal development, it is so important to be committed to your goal. This may seem obvious, but I've come across many people who said they wanted something, and then came to realize they didn't want it badly enough to be 100% committed. Or they didn't want it enough to make the necessary sacrifices in order to achieve it.

Let's get clear now. On a scale of 1-10, how committed are you to finding a new career path? If your answer is not a 10, what do you need to change to make it a 10?

Write down your answer and decide what you will do about boosting your level of commitment to a 10. Will it take more research, more reflection, perhaps talking to a friend? Will you make a list of pros and cons? Choose any action that will help you clarify the degree of your desire and commitment. Write down the action in your Career Journal.

Your Commitment Statement

You've heard the saying, "It's not real until it's in writing." It applies here too. You are now ready to make an agreement with yourself in your Career Journal. I agree to:

- Make this a priority in my life.
- Be honest and open.

- Be willing to self-reflect, even in the hard-to-look places.
- Be okay with not knowing answers to some questions.
- Be like a kid in a candy store—open to possibilities and ideas I've never thought of before.

_____

SIGNATURE   DATE

Next, identify your commitment. Be as specific as you can. An example might be: "I'm committed to finding a career I love and taking action toward creating it within the next four months." Or "I'm committed to finding out if I really want to be a small business owner, and I'm open to whatever answer I find."

My Commitment

_____

_____

_____

_____

_____

Post Your Commitment Agreement Somewhere
You Will See It Every Day

Place it in your planner, on your bathroom mirror or refrigerator—anywhere you will see it every day to remind you of your commitment. Looking at this every day will help you stay motivated and focused.

Step 2: Setting The Right Goals

This goal setting process will help you stick to your plan without feeling overwhelmed by a sense of vagueness that comes with nonspecific answers to "How am I going to get there?" Initial goal setting is a must. Don't skim over this practical process. Without it, you'll likely wander aimlessly, merely wishing and hoping for something better, instead of moving on with your career transition and actually getting what you want.

Start by establishing the right goals. By this I mean, make them *specific*, *tangible*, and *measurable*. Be sure to include a timeframe as well. Your goals should be realistic, but they should also be a bit of a stretch so that you're pushing yourself beyond what you'd normally do in order to move forward.

Ask yourself, "Where am I going? What is my ultimate goal?" Write down your answer.

Now start brainstorming about how you're going to get there. Write these ideas down.

If you're still not clear, that's okay. Just get started, and things will fall into place as you go. Clarity itself is a process.

For example, when your mind is feeling creative and unrestrained, you might write down a goal or career objective that sounds something like this:

Quit my job, open health food store.

This is a great starting point and indeed a career goal to aspire to. However, you can see that you still need a practical working plan to carry out this goal, along with a timeframe to make it happen. Does this mean the goal is not good? Not at all. Keep this as your Master Goal: *Quit my job, open a health food store.* Then you will create smaller, practical sub-goals that you can fulfill in order to reach this major milestone in your professional life.

You will also find that the best plans often manifest themselves in outline form. Beneath the umbrella goal of "Quit my job, open a health food store," you might list a series of sub-goals. These could be:

1. Start a savings plan.
2. Further my business education.
3. Look into real estate possibilities for a future store.
4. Do informational interviews—talk to others who own health food stores or franchises.

Notice that these career goals still do not meet the requirement of being tangible, measurable, and time-sensitive. You now need to zoom in even closer on your goals to make them more specific.

Let's look at sub-goal 1: "Start a savings plan." Here, you can break this down into stepping-stone goals, which could be:

1. Set up an investment plan with financial advisor that will allow me to accumulate savings of a specific amount that I can dip into and use within a year. Deadline for goal: Nov. 15.

2. Redesign household budget plan. Make cuts in some areas to set aside a surplus of $1,000 (for example) to be invested in savings for future business. Deadline for goal: Nov. 15.

As you can see, once you break down the larger goals into smaller, feasible sub-goals that can be achieved by a certain time, you can then determine how long it will take to achieve all the sub-goals. Once you've established the timeframe for sub-goals, you can then assign a long-term deadline to your Master Goal, in this example, that of owning a health food store.

An important note about goals: As you move past obstacles in your career path and graduate to the next steps, you may be forced to do some goal rewriting. Know that this is okay, it is a natural part of the process. You can be flexible and you get to change your goals as needed.

You're in charge.

Step 3: Creating and Writing Your Transition Plan

Before you can move past the point of vague possibilities and enter the process of a serious career change, you'll need to develop a transition plan that covers the financial, mental, and emotional aspects of your life based on the goals you have identified. This is an especially critical step because you support yourself and feel the need to rely on yourself first and foremost.

Here's the good news: You *can* rely on yourself. Know that you are strong and capable enough to lean on yourself. Plus, you have a lot of freedom here to carve out your dream career and make necessary changes along the way. You are flexible and nimble with plenty of options.

The basics of your plan should include the following[5]:

1. Financial

Budget Your Monthly Bills. Ask your bank for a budgeting worksheet or find one online to help you get organized with handling your basic monthly expenses. Factor in the mortgage or rent, school loans, utilities, car insurance, car payments, and/or other transportation. Include groceries, gas money, childcare, personal items, wardrobe, home expenses, and so forth. Tally all the basics, and don't forget to

[5] *I Can't Believe I Get Paid To Do This!* by Stacey Mayo

put aside a bit for entertainment. You deserve and need to have some fun along the way.

Make Cutbacks Where Needed. Review your credit card bills, checkbook, bank statements, and receipts. Determine where you are spending your money each month. Decide what items you can either cross off the list entirely or find ways to scale back. Then, take an inventory of the places you have spent money in the last few months. Place them into categories and prioritize them according to importance. Now go down the list and determine where you can cut back without feeling like you're depriving yourself.

Start a Savings Plan Devoted To Your Career Transition. Open a savings account devoted entirely to your new professional endeavor. If part of your plan includes action steps that require funding, a special account is the best way to begin funding it. For example, you may wish to talk to a financial advisor to learn the most sensible ways to invest your money while planning for the not-so-long term. Or if you're starting a new business or going back to school, you may want to investigate business loans, student loan applications, grants, or scholarship possibilities.

2. Mental

Develop Your Skills. If you were to schedule an interview for your dream job tomorrow, would you be ready with the necessary skills to land the position? If not, make a list of the skills you'll need to acquire for your new career path and include the most cost-effective way to obtain them within your desired timeframe. Then, develop specific goals for each skill and a timeframe in which you will complete them. For example, include the length of time you'll need to complete a class you need to take.

Get Additional Career Questions Answered. Take time to define what elements of your dream career you still don't fully understand. There probably are a few since it's new for you. That's okay. As with any other new endeavor you've undertaken, you can get the information and knowledge you need. Take advantage of the free resources out there first. Surf the Internet, go to the library, or talk to trusted experts. If you need to invest in additional resources, weigh the pros and cons. Make sure the investment will get you to where you want to go and is worth your time and money.

Reward Yourself. Reward yourself for milestones you achieve along the way. This is a time for encouragement, confidence, and a can-do attitude. It helps to "feed your hungry mind" what it needs to grow spiritually, intellectually, and professionally. Read inspirational books, listen to your favorite music. It helps tremendously to surround yourself with whatever feels uplifting to you and reinforces a positive attitude.

3. Emotional

Manage Negative Voices. The emotional aspect of career change is one of the most important to address because your emotions, fears, and negative beliefs can be your biggest obstacles. Singles sometimes grapple with feelings of loneliness. Remember that you are never alone. Relief often comes in the form of understanding peers, career buddies who are going through the same changes as you are, a career coach who can help steady your course as you make the transition, or just the patient listening of a good friend. For some, self-help books and counseling also can help ease the doubts and fears.

In the Dreaming First phase, I suggested completely ignoring the negative voices. This was important in order to allow you to dream and dream BIG, unencumbered by negative thoughts. In this stage, creating your transition plan, it's important to begin actively managing your negative voices rather than just pushing them aside. Notice when they speak to you. What do they say? If anything they're saying is actually true, such as you tend to procrastinate on tasks, include a way to handle this obstacle in your transition plan. Take action, then let the rest of the negative voice go. Don't engage in extensive dialogue with them but notice when they pop up and the things they tend to say repeatedly to you.

Create a plan for managing your negative voices so they aren't running the show. For example, ignore them when they come up and focus instead on something positive that makes you feel good or take a walk outside to clear your head. In the Recommended Resources section I suggest purchasing a copy of *Taming Your Gremlin.* Using the tips in this book can help you keep those negative thoughts at bay. Find the best way to manage your negative voices and use them on a regular basis. I'll mention negative voices again because they are one of the biggest obstacles people encounter during career transition.

Step 4: Putting the Puzzle Together Piece by Piece

· ·

The Secret To Finding The Right Job. Sometimes finding the right job or career can seem like a very big puzzle. But even the most intricate puzzle can be completed piece-by-piece, one step at a time. However, many of us want to know every single step we need to take to land the perfect job in advance. And we want all pieces to fit in exact sequence. Often, we won't even take the first step until we have the entire path mapped out. Somehow it feels safer that way. Sound familiar?

Unfortunately, neither life nor career transition usually works out that neatly. There is no one-size-fits-all road map for finding the perfect job.

So when my clients want to know all of the steps before getting started, I suggest we first start putting the puzzle together piece-by-piece. Once an idea begins to form, we move in that direction. For you, I suggest:

- Follow your gut instinct.
- Take a step in a direction that feels right.
- Allow yourself the freedom to explore options as you move forward.

Part of this process is trusting that you'll be able to figure out how best to make the transition as you go. You just need to take a step in one direction and things will become clearer; then, as you take another step, things become even more clear, and so on, until the puzzle emerges as the full

picture and you find your dream job. You've heard it before: it is a process, a journey. For some it's short; for others
it may take a little longer. It just depends on your starting
point and your willingness to keep on stepping.

Tips to 'Keep On Stepping'

Keep up-to-date on your dream career. Continue doing
your career homework. Visit the library, local stores, or
check out online bookstores for resources about the career
field you want to enter. Stay up to date by reading the business section in your local newspaper. You never know when
you'll find just the right person or company to connect with
in your own hometown.

Start looking for a mentor. Be on the watch for someone who does what you think you might want to do. Is
there a friend or family member who works in your field
you could talk to? Identify someone who's been there, done
that, and is successful in the field you want to pursue. Consider whether this person could be a good mentor for you
and reach out to see if it's a fit. You may approach several
people to see who is the best fit for you and who has the
time to help you along your way. Set up some time to talk
with them about your goals and ask them to tell you about
their career path. Ask about the preparation they needed to
get a foot in the door, how they spent their early days, and
how they spend their days now. Ask about the most important lessons they learned along the way that contributed
to their success. People are often generous with their time

when asked to share their experience. Even if one person doesn't end up being your mentor, having that first meeting can provide you with valuable tips and tools for breaking into your new career field.

Take a class or two. Research and sign up for continuing education or community classes to learn more about your dream career. You can get the information you need by checking regularly in the newspaper, visiting college websites, or calling/showing up to find out what is being offered through the local school system or universities. If you don't have educational resources nearby, try online classes. There are many distance learning online classes designed especially for students unable to attend on-campus programs or who live in rural areas.

Conduct informational interviews. Set up a time to speak to someone in your chosen field, so that you may learn what it is really like to work in that field, and learn about possible career opportunities. This is similar to finding a mentor, however, not everyone will become your mentor. It's helpful to learn as much as you can about your chosen field through people who are already there. They are the ones who know your industry in and out. So conduct as many informational interviews as you can. And keep an eye out for someone who's taken a special interest in you and may be willing to be your mentor.

There are many ways to land an informational interview. You might begin by speaking to someone in your social circle who already has a foot in the door. You could scan online for companies that appeal to you, and then ask if you can schedule an informational interview with someone in their office. You could even suggest one with a family member who works in a position or with a company that appeals to you.

Networking. Find local associations for your career field. Network with family and friends, let them know you're looking to make a change. Nothing beats live, in-person communication. But you can also utilize online career networking in addition to in-person networking events. The web is a good place to meet professionals who are searching for your brand of talent. For more information about networking for singles, see the Networking for Singles bonus section at the end of this book.

Be a career opportunist. Look for volunteer opportunities that will give you experience in your area of interest. There's no better way to find out what it's really like to work in a specific field than to jump in feet first as a volunteer. At the very least, you can get a letter of recommendation once you've completed your volunteer program. If you are working toward a degree, take advantage of internship opportunities available through your university. Many corporations have ongoing relationships with universities and colleges that allow you to earn internship credit hours.

Take a break. If you are currently working, consider taking a sabbatical, hiatus, or a vacation to try something new. You can use the time to explore an entirely different profession, do in-depth career research, or try out something new part-time. You could even relax and have some fun. Remarkable ideas have been know to manifest under the most pleasant, unexpected circumstances.

Remember, it's more important to just get started than it is to wait until you've developed a perfectly planned course of action. If you wait for things to be perfect, you could be waiting a very long time.

4

Small Sacrifices, Big Rewards
Remaining Financially Stable During Transition

A major part of planning for your career transition is deciding how you will manage your finances during the change. You need to take care of your bills; that's a given. It's hard to dream and plan for the future when you're concerned about paying the bills. You need to be practical and determine what your options are for becoming and remaining financially stable during your transition.

It's important to keep in mind that there are many different ways to go about making this change. There is no one way. You just need to find a solution that works best for you. Here are some possibilities that will help you brainstorm more ways to keep yourself financially viable:

- *Possibility 1:* Stay in your current position and work on the next career step after hours and on weekends.

- *Possibility 2:* Start saving. Begin to set aside savings that will allow you to cover at least three months of living expenses to provide you with the freedom to begin a new career.
- *Possibility 3:* Find a part-time job that pays enough to cover your bills and work on your dream job after hours. This is what I did during my career change; it worked extremely well.
- *Possibility 4:* Go back to school part-time, in the evenings, or on weekends to gain the education you will need to advance in your new career.
- *Possibility 5:* It is also completely okay to find a job doing the same thing you are doing now, but one that involves less stress or fewer work hours so that you have more time and energy to focus on your career search. Some people see this as a step back and that just isn't so. Consider it a transition job that is serving a purpose—the purpose of keeping you financially stable while you pursue your dream.

No matter what you decide, keep your options open and be willing to make changes as needed. Don't put too much pressure on yourself to make the perfect choice. Remember, there are many ways to make the transition. Here are more tips to help you figure things out:

Figure out what works for you and be willing to make small, temporary sacrifices. If you decide to find another job that pays your bills and allows you greater freedom to pursue the next career path, it's okay if your temporary position isn't incredibly rewarding. You need to enjoy it on some level but it's not the end all be all. It's serving a purpose. Find something that's easy to do, so you have energy at night or in your down time to devote to the new endeavor.

Working nine-to-five is not the only way. There are many ways to generate income. Working eight hours a day, nine-to-five is not the only way. One of my clients decided to pursue her passion of freelance writing after hours, while working in a human resources position. Another client found her passion in a franchise business that she now runs. She saved up some of the required franchise money, and then got a loan for the rest to get started.

In both cases, they made temporary sacrifices in order to pursue their dreams. One involved a sacrifice of time to work on her new business after hours, and the other required a financial sacrifice by saving her money and then taking out a loan for the balance of the investment. Both found the sacrifices well worth it because it allowed them to pursue and accomplish their career dreams. When I look back on the sacrifices I made during my career transition, they seem miniscule compared to the fulfillment I now feel in having achieved my dream career.

Reprioritize spending habits. We've discussed basic monthly budgeting, but it is also important to reprioritize your spending habits so you can factor in the items you'll need to pursue your dream. Things like specialized training, computer courses, books, software, career coaching, and special interest memberships all cost money. Of course, the amount you spend will vary depending on your personal spending habits and priorities.

First, make sure you feel financially free enough to confidently add "Career Seeking Pursuits" to your list of monthly expenditures. If you don't, take some time to consider what steps you can take to get there so you can forge ahead with confidence. For example, set aside a certain amount of money each month in savings so that you feel more financially secure. Brainstorm another way to bring in extra income, like freelancing on the side as we've discussed earlier. Or decide where you can cut back on your spending in one area, and funnel those funds toward your career seeking endeavors.

Be patient with yourself. It took me about three years from the time I left my position as a marketing and communications specialist to creating a full-time coaching practice. While I grew my practice, I chose to take a part-time job that paid my basic bills. The process took time, effort and commitment. And there were plenty of days when I wanted things to move more quickly, but I would do it again in a heartbeat. So stay focused and committed. In the end, it will pay off for you, too.

Married to Your Bank Account

In Chapter One we discussed being married to your current job or career. Carry that analogy a bit further and consider what happens when you're married to your bank account. You may have developed somewhat of a codependent relationship with your current financial situation without realizing it. You may expect a certain amount of money to always be there, no matter what, or you may be in the habit of prorating some expenses to a later paycheck. This can happen to anyone, and it's a problem because it can keep you stuck in a job you don't like.

Some people develop earning and spending patterns that form the basis of a vicious cycle. You bring home your monthly salary with the full intention of putting it toward specified expenditures, such as savings, rent, utilities, food, and other basics. But after those expenses are paid, you begin chipping away at your credit card debt, based on the notion that you will apply your forthcoming paycheck/income toward that debt. This is why so many live paycheck-to-paycheck and news reports reflect that more Americans are building large credit card debt betting on future "pay it later" income, which often doesn't come. This has become much the norm in today's society. There are numerous contributing factors, some extraordinary, such as unexpected emergency repairs or medical expenses, but most have to do with routine spending habits.

Let's say this scenario loosely defines your attitude toward money. As you grew into your independence, you likely developed a set pattern of habits and behaviors that became the norm for you. Maybe you go out for an expensive lunch twice a week with friends. Perhaps you pay a monthly fee for a social club or treat yourself to concerts, movies, or other social engagements each week. Maybe you even take a couple of expensive vacations each year or purchase new clothes when you don't really need them.

Nothing out of the ordinary, you may say. And there's nothing wrong with this. But you need to look at whether your spending is a factor that could hold you back from making a career change. If your spending keeps you stuck in a job that isn't a fit, something needs to change. You'll need to consider whether you want to stay married to your bank account and attached to that large paycheck, even though you're unfulfilled at your job. If you're ready to break the cycle and progress with a new plan to achieve financial security and fulfillment in your career, you can start right now.

Take another look at the numbers. Narrow down expenses even further. Look at the things you put your hard-earned salary toward. Take a look at your credit card bills again. Now consider giving up one, two, or three of those things so that you can make room for a different set of financial responsibilities.

This may not be easy at first. Or, it sounds like it could be easy in theory but when you actually try to do it, you get stuck spinning your wheels, unable to move ahead with your plan. That's okay, it's normal; and it needs to change. This is a sign that you have become unwilling to compromise with your bank account, reluctant to allow new priorities to govern your spending.

Identify Your Money Blocks

Recognize your financial handicaps and mental money blocks. You can go beyond them and develop a solid plan to support yourself financially during career transition. You can learn to problem-solve your money blocks and invest for your future career success while removing the blocks. Once you eliminate your blocks—your misconceptions about money—you'll move ahead with greater ease.

Major Money Misconceptions

Imagine what would happen in your career and life if you shook off *all* of your negative attitudes about money. See if any of the following resonate with you.

Money Misconception 1: **It's All On Me.**

See if this sounds familiar: "A career change translates to lean times ahead, and that's something I can't handle right now. I am the sole income earner, so there is no one else to support me financially. I feel protective and sometimes even defensive when talking about my money issues."

One thing that we can all relate to in life is money. We have all felt dependent on money to some extent, small or large, at different points in our lives, and we have all made mistakes involving money. The lessons someone else has learned and grown from can be beneficial to your financial future, provided you are willing to listen with an open mind and are eager to make the change.

Yes, you are ultimately responsible to support and take care of yourself, but there is a world full of good people out there, many of whom are willing to offer advice and even expert counsel. In many cases, your family members will be able to lend insightful perspectives on investing and saving money—if you give them a chance. They may surprise you by being much more understanding than you might imagine. However, if being too close for comfort keeps your family from remaining objective, you can always talk to a third party: a career coach, mentor, or another type of advisor who can help you sort things out. A third party can then make recommendations on what to do and who to contact next.

If you're struggling to get out of debt, remember that a financial expert will work with you to consolidate your bills and develop payment schedules that you will feel comfortable with. A reputable investment professional will offer unbiased input and teach you to be wise about wealth building. Sometimes the easiest thing to do is to ask a friend for a qualified referral. You could also take out a loan with a reasonable payment timeframe so that you have extra income to devote toward your career transition. As a single person, yes you are independent, however, in no way does this mean you are stuck shouldering your financial burdens alone.

Although it may feel like "It's all on me," remember that there are people out there willing to lend advice and to give you a helping hand. Shift your thinking around money toward something more positive like, "I can make this happen and I can get the help I need. I am financially successful and can take care of myself. I have the freedom right now of being single and I'm able to make any choice I want."

Money Misconception 2: I Can't Afford a Career Change.

You might be saying, "My current salary covers every aspect of my lifestyle. I've worked hard to get to the place in life where I am today, and I enjoy living life the way I like. I don't think there is any room for one more expense, so my dreams of a more fulfilling career will have to wait." In other words: you think you can't afford it.

Many single career seekers hold "I can't afford it," as a prime belief and it keeps them stuck in unfulfilling jobs for years. They're bound to their current lifestyles and entirely dependent upon paychecks. "I can't afford it" is something I frequently hear from frustrated clients who want to break out of their career rut but feel shaky on the money part of things. This negative belief in lack is simply not so.

Any prosperity teacher will tell you that you've got to take risks with what you have before you can master the art of attracting more. It's an essential part of the abundance mindset and the world's wealthiest people know this. It's not a secret; they speak about it, write books about it, and sell their wealth-building strategies openly in the market-place. You can learn and benefit greatly from the world's richest people, but that doesn't mean being reckless or fool-hardy about your money. It means taking full control of your money situation and recognizing that nothing in your life is set in stone.

If you're willing to compromise in some areas, you will be able to take the necessary financial steps toward investing in your career. The trick though is to develop the willingness to compromise along with the determination to overcome obstacles. If you want a new career badly enough, you will find ways to maneuver around any obstacles that keep you from it. If you lead a very socially active or "full" lifestyle, then those financial obstacles are most likely self-erected. This means that you can definitely chip away at them one by one without compromising too much of "the good life." You'll find a way to work around them without feeling deprived.

Money Misconception 3:
Scrimping and Saving are Lonely Activities.

When you first embark on a plan to start saving money, you may feel the pinch of not having that extra cash at your disposal. You also might feel a bit isolated from your pals while you are busy concentrating on your new career.

Some singles think that they will lose their friends or sacrifice their social lives if they have to restrict spending in favor of career pursuits. But sometimes being more selective about whom you choose to spend time (and money) with can be a very good thing. If you tell your friends in a nice way, "I'm on a budget right now because I'm starting my own business," (or going back to school) don't be surprised if they are not only understanding of your goals but supportive of your cause.

We have all been that person struggling to turn over a new leaf, financially or otherwise. If your friends are true friends, they will be there for you no matter what. And don't be surprised when they decide to treat you to dinner or a movie, just to let you know you're appreciated while you're going through your transition.

Finally, for those who feel saving equates to deprivation, shift your focus to the future rather than dwelling on what you don't have or what you are doing without. Imagine instead the incredible sense of accomplishment and personal satisfaction you will experience when you are that much closer to having the career of your dreams.

• • • • •

The reality is that there is nothing more fulfilling than self-betterment. Learning something new, embarking on a personal journey and discovering what you were meant to do with your life is truly being in control of your life—now and for your future. This knowledge alone will overshadow any small sacrifices you need to make along the way.

When you shift your priorities toward achieving your dream career, you won't mind making the sacrifices as much because you're working toward doing something you love.

Keep your eye on the long-term goal and you'll soon realize that it's okay to go out once or twice a month instead of once or twice a week. It depends on what works for you, but know that it will get easier because you are working toward long term career fulfillment. This is incredibly motivating and empowering.

Instead of focusing on how much money you don't have, take care of your bills and focus your time and attention on what you want and what you *do have*. I know this from using the principles of *Law of Attraction* described in the movie *The Secret* in which we're told that what you focus on expands. Now ask yourself what do you want to expand? You don't want to give more energy expansion to money misconceptions, but it's important to recognize which misconception you most relate to—It's All On Me, I Can't Afford It, or Saving Is Lonely.

Ask how many of these scenarios could be holding you back from financial stability and the freedom to change jobs, to go back to school, or start your own business.

Which misconceptions are you willing to let go of? Decide this now. It will expand your possibilities and move you forward.

Become and Remain Financially Stable

Now that you have identified the money issues and misconceptions that may have wedged themselves between you and your freedom, let's switch gears and talk about becoming truly financially stable for your career's sake.

It must be your goal to move out of the red zone and into a place where you can begin putting away money toward your future professional pursuits. While not everybody makes a career transition from a financially abundant place, it helps to feel as comfortable and secure as possible about your money situation before you set your more specific goals.

Pull out your monthly budget sheet, the one you completed in Chapter Three:

Review your basic expenses, then identify your short and long-term financial goals. For example, how will you pay your monthly bills in the short term, and what will you do to cover those bills and pay for your career transition for the long term? (This may seem like an obvious step, but when my coach asked me years ago how much I needed to live each month, I did not know!)

Next, review your plan for loans, savings, and support from parents, other family members, or a partner in your career endeavor.

A good way to set this plan in motion is to stop worrying about where the money will come from, or thinking "What if I can't pay back my debts?" Instead, operate from a confident place within you. Tell yourself, "I will make this happen. And if whatever I'm currently doing isn't working for me, I know that there are always other options. I just have to find the right one for my situation."

Lifestyle and the Art of Financial Compromise

Earlier in this chapter, we touched upon the single lifestyle and the price tag attached to many activities typical for singles. No matter what your personality, set of hobbies, and other interests are, you may spend a substantial amount of money on leisure activities each month. Making a successful career transition means setting goals and managing your finances, but unless you have a large stockpile of savings at your disposal, a career change may require a more frugal mentality than perhaps you are used to. If you do have money saved up for at least three to four months of living expenses, that's great and you won't have to worry as much about cutting expenses.

But if you do not have enough saved up, which is the category most people fall into, some specific, concrete money saving tips can help you spend less while still enjoying your single lifestyle. Compromise is possible and not as painful as you might think.

Money Saving Tips for Singles

Entertainment:

- Reduce dining out to once per week, or every other week if you want to save even more.
- Rent or buy DVDs instead of going to the movies. Watch what's on TV, or invite friends over for a movie night.
- Limit yourself to one or two outings per month and one "expensive" trip per season.
- Devote at least one weekend day to following up on your career research and transition plan instead of attending expensive social outings.
- Opt for sports on TV instead of buying expensive tickets to live games.
- Take advantage of your hometown athletics—football, soccer, baseball, hockey, and more.
- Turn down the really swank affairs for now and put that money toward your new career. Politely explain to friends that you're on a budget. Good friends usually understand because they've been there.

Food:

- Create a meal plan and make weekly trips to the supermarket to stock up instead of buying your lunch and dinner out every day.
- Pack lunches the night before work so you can "grab and go" in the morning.
- Do easy crock-pot dinners.
- Store extra portions and leftovers in the freezer. Thaw in the morning or use a microwave to heat them up for lunch or dinner.

Physical Fitness & Exercise:

- Quit the gym temporarily while in transition, but don't stop exercising. Take advantage of free hiking trails, community centers, local parks, and recreation facilities that do not require membership fees.
- Instead of going to the gym, rent exercise tapes, such as Tae-Bo, Pilates, yoga, and aerobics. While you're exercising, envision the perfect career for you and the steps you will take to get there.
- Walk, jog, or bike outdoors—for free!
- Invest in/ask for exercise equipment for holidays and birthdays (free weights, stepper, treadmill).

Business/Office/Career Expenses:

- Scour Craigslist.org and Ebay.com for the best deals on new and used computer equipment or anything else you might need.

- Keep an eye out for open source and freeware. You can get many computer programs free or inexpensively online if you know where to look.
- Assess the value of all paid sites you belong to and quit membership sites that you pay for and don't use.
- Downgrade memberships where possible.
- Join a few new (and free) career sites as a way to further your knowledge of the field you'd like to pursue. Many sites offer free memberships with great features.
- Purchase used equipment at a reduced rate instead of paying full price for new equipment.
- If you're shopping for career clothing, hit the big sales or shop at discount stores.

Other:
- Choose frugal gifts from the heart—such as a photo album or frame with photos you add yourself.
- Hang on to your most cherished hobbies and limit your spending on other hobbies.

5

How to Get Off the Roller Coaster
Emotional Support Especially for Singles

How you're feeling at any particular time can make or break your progress.

No matter what stage of career transition you're in, one thing is certain: Emotions will play a significant role. For men and women who don't have a partner to lean on, this can be especially tough. Sometimes you feel overly sensitive about things you know aren't be a big deal, but to you they are all consuming. This can dampen your enthusiasm and keep you from achieving what you want, but you don't have to fall into the trap of being at the mercy of your negative thoughts or feelings.

Learn that emotions are natural and accept that feelings come and go. The trick is to let them ebb and flow while keeping a healthy perspective and feeling good about yourself and your plan for the future. When you accept feelings as a natural flow, you can maintain perspective more easily, even in the midst of emotional turbulence.

In general, when you're emotionally vulnerable you have trouble focusing on your new career path and the end result. This chapter is dedicated to all the single career seekers I have helped find relief from the emotional roller coaster and uncover the answers within themselves. I want to help you do the same. Yes, you *can* have your emotional needs met while continuing to strive toward your career goals. At times it may seem like a hard road to travel, but believe it when I say that anything is possible. You can do and be what you want.

First and foremost, please know that all emotions are perfectly normal—normal to feel and healthy to acknowledge. So many people feel guilty about having certain feelings. They look for ways to block them out, or they bury them beneath layers of rationalizations. Instead, be glad that you are able to feel deeply and wholly. Vulnerability is part of being human.

The 'I Ain't Got Nobody' Affliction

At times, each of us has experienced the "I ain't got nobody" affliction. For singles, this can come up with perturbing regularity. And, we often perceive our aloneness as loneliness, but these are two different things. Aloneness simply means being alone, or being single without a partner. Male or female, the feeling of loneliness, however, can prevent you from having what you want. If you stay in the feeling too long, it will get you stuck.

Remember, you are never really alone. There are kindred souls just like you going through similar challenges, and there are family members, friends, mentors, as well as people you have yet to meet who have "been there and done that." They will be able to steer you in the right direction *if you just let them know* how you are feeling and what you need help with. You'll soon find someone who can help steady you along your course with sound advice and a practical plan that's based on your dream of the perfect career.

Share selectively. Once you have started to develop your transition plan, it's time to start sharing your plan with those kindred souls who will be supportive. Since you are more solid in your plan, those you ask for support and guidance will be too. Share selectively, however. I recommend choosing people who you know won't dismiss your plans or diminish your enthusiasm. Again, this keeps negative voices at bay.

Emotions run in cycles. Emotional patterns typically run in cycles—bursts of confidence, energy, and high output often followed by down cycles flooded with doubt, fear, and indecision. Being aware of your own patterns is key to managing the ups and downs. It does, however, take some practice. When the emotional tide runs high, you can learn how to navigate through these rough waters and you will recover faster, feel more at peace with yourself, and be ready to tackle the next phase of career transition with a sense of purpose, determination, and greater confidence. Like taking a white water rafting trip, the first trip might have had you fighting to get the right paddling rhythm, but by your second trip you start to get the hang of moving through the rapids.

Emotions can bring about profound change. Emotions are often the prelude to profound change and spiritual growth. They're your mind's way of trying to protect you or tell you that you need something. Don't deny yourself an emotional release by hiding from emotions. Approach your feelings from an inquisitive point of view. What is your mind asking for? Take some time to consider what you need in the moment, and then find a way to get it. If it's an emotional release you need, go outside and exercise. If you're confused and frustrated, try journaling about your thoughts. See what comes out. You'll be surprised at what you discover just by getting it down on paper.

Emotions can help you release stress. Emotions are also the body's way of releasing stress. They are signals worth watching. Stress relief is an important part of career transition and good health in general. So, even if at times you feel you're spilling over with emotion, don't panic. Instead, learn to acknowledge your emotions when they surface, harness them to help you get where you need to be, and then do what you need to do to take care of yourself.

Emotional Obstacles and Pick-Me-Ups

The more you learn to overcome obstacles throughout your journey, the better. And, many obstacles you face may continue to come up at different levels of intensity so you'll want to be prepared for them and have a few "pick-me-ups" on hand.

Emotional Obstacle 1: **All on you, no way out.** I discuss the feeling of shouldering one's own emotional burdens, the feeling of "It's all on me" throughout the book. Why? Because this feeling continues to come up with the ebb and flow of your career transition, especially for singles. Whether you are a single mom or dad with kids to support, or responsible only for yourself, you may still feel it's all on you and there's no way out. Remember, you don't have to stay in a dead-end job that makes you miserable. You can be proactive and seek out the financial and emotional support you need at any given time.

To know yourself and what makes you happy; to know that you don't have to be seduced by an illusion that the paycheck alone is responsible for your happiness is a wonderful feeling. Only then can you find a way to turn illusion into profit by way of making your new career happen with greater clarity. Now that's exciting.

Emotional Obstacle 2: **Tough to manage current job tasks and keep up with career homework.** Maybe you are aware of this condition—a busy work schedule, fluctuating energy levels and resulting procrastination. Here's how it plays out:

You wake up Monday morning inspired and ready to dive in with some solid plans. You sail through your tasks at work, enjoy a good lunch, make plans for the weekend, and head home at the end of the day with career searching on the brain. After a quick workout and a healthy dinner, it's on to the computer for some research into your field of interest.

You locate some great new websites, send out a few e-mails reaching out to potential career-seeking friends whom you've met online, and then follow up with a financial advisor your best friend told you about. By bedtime, you feel like you've accomplished just what you wanted in the day. You drift off with visions of your perfect career dancing happily in your head.

Fast forward through the week. Communication at your workplace has escalated to a feverish pitch. Your current job takes its toll and things get so busy that you don't make time for your career search. This can happen easily, but you need to make time no matter what tasks or emergencies come up. Too often, when Friday rolls around, you check off all that's on your to-do list at work but you haven't gotten to your career transition action items. New career follow-ups? That's the last thing on your mind. You are tired, feeling complacent, perhaps irritated, and entirely unmotivated to tackle something new. The week has taken its toll.

At the end of a hectic work week, fatigue and wondering where the time went are normal reactions. Simply make a plan to manage your time differently the next week. Remember, only you can make your career transition tasks priorities. Decide on what times would work out better for you. It may be best to work on your career change twice a week for two hours, on your lunch break, or some other plan that allows you to be fresh of mind when you're doing it. Whatever time you choose, *mark it on your calendar*.

A quick way to help you prioritize is to go back to the commitment agreement you made in Chapter Three. Re-

read it for inspiration, and then decide how you will get reorganized and embark on a new weekly plan that works out better. Be flexible. Not all weeks are equal in emotional and work-related velocity, but your new time schedule may be just the right choice that turns into a positive habit and enables you to maintain a higher level of motivation.

Know when to ask for help and support. I'm guessing a lot of career seekers relate to the end-of-the-week blues because this is simply how the rhythm of life sometimes goes. For singles, however, there is no immediate partner who can pat you on the back and tell you everything will work out all right. This is why you have to learn to ask for help. If you have trouble asking for what you want, you can learn to overcome your resistance by just trying it a few times. You'll be glad you've kicked the habit of not asking when you discover how delighted most people are to lend an ear, and often some fine, practical counsel.

If you had a tough week and your energy level took a nosedive that's okay. Some days you are exhausted—mentally and emotionally. This is not, however, a good reason to stay immersed in dismal thoughts. These times occur for everyone. At times like these, it often helps to flash back to your finer moments, times you succeeded in the past, then look ahead with confidence to your future plans.

Should a difficult week or anything else derail you, take another look at the transition plan itself. Is your transition plan strong enough to weather the tough weeks, or is it weak on details? If your plan doesn't map out the tangibles and what you want to accomplish within a particular timeframe, it's easy to get distracted and lose sight of where you're going. Does your plan allow for contingencies like those tough weeks?

Review your plan again and make the necessary altera-tions. "Reset" your plan and then schedule where you know you are going to be during the course of several days. Your new career tasks will be easier to accomplish. Soon they will become automatic, like a *good* habit. Also, you will have less time to dwell on unexpected setbacks. Before you real-ize it, you will have made significant strides forward.

Exercise: Instant Emotional Energy Pick-Me-Ups

. . . .

This exercise comes in handy for those times when you feel a bit down or like a victim in your current situation.

Write down or imagine your responses to the following:

1. Right now I feel _____
    (describe emotion) because:

2. What I really wish would happen is (feel free to drift into a fantasy scenario here):

3. The last time someone said something really nice about me was (describe what they said exactly):

4. I am most proud of my ability/abilities to (elaborate if you like):

5. I can help myself to feel better right now if I:

   • Call or e-mail a friend or family member
   • Do something I intended to get done, but didn't
   • Make a specific plan to go out tomorrow
   • Clean my house and/or get my office organized

- Do something creative—write, paint, sculpt, etc.
- Listen to relaxing music or watch a good movie on TV
- Other

Choose one or two from above and then do it.

1. I vow to get right back into my career-seeking saddle and work on the following tangible goals next week:

Goal _____

Deadline _____

Goal _____

Deadline _____

Goal _____

Deadline _____

Tips for Handling Loneliness

- **Permit yourself to experience loneliness from time to time.** It's a normal emotion. As humans we crave contact and we all have the desire to be understood. If you feel lonely, it may be a sign that it's time to reach out to some new places and faces.

- **Read books or listen to audiotapes.** Include inspiring stories from people who have made it happen for themselves. Visualize yourself creating a similar situation in your own career and life.
- **Gain inspiration from people in your life.** Choose people who have made their dreams happen. Reach out to family members, friends, online contacts, and others. Don't be afraid to introduce yourself to someone new.

Emotional Obstacle 3: **My friends aren't being supportive.** How many times has this happened? You're out to dinner with friends when suddenly the conversation turns to work. It doesn't take long before complaints start flying. The entire table dishes their share of bad boss stories, obnoxious coworkers or hard work with poor pay. But as human as commiserating may be, this version of "Ain't It Awful" works against you. And it needs to stop. Engaging in this kind of negative talk will not help you move forward. By commiserating you are focusing on what you don't want. You want to focus on what you *do want.*

At first, this may not be easy because it may be a different dynamic in thinking for you. It takes practice to change negative talk and thoughts, especially when you're among others who are focused primarily on the negative. It may be difficult for you to be that person who is ready to think and speak differently, ready to take risks, and choose a path other than the status quo.

People seem to want to follow the herd more often than choosing to break out with their own plans in pursuit of their dreams. This is also why it can be difficult to get support from the herd. It may make you feel uncomfortable about divulging your idea of doing something great like starting your own business, going back to school, or trying for a new type of position in a different field than the one they've always identified you as being in.

What should you do? You've probably guessed it: start a new herd. You're going to establish a new support network, but you're going to call it something else—your Dream Team. In the next chapter you'll begin building your Dream Team. Get ready for your world to get bigger and your career transition to get a whole lot easier.

6

Building Your Dream Team
Your Career Transition MVPs

It is vital to have a support network during career transition, though sometimes the people in your career support network are not those who make up your usual circle of friends. This can feel a bit strange at first, but you'll soon grow accustomed to talking in-depth about your career plans with these valuable players, and to guarding your dreams from doubters, naysayers, and anyone who might bring you down for whatever reason.

Who is going to be on your Career Seeker's Dream Team? Let's set it up. This is where your life gets bigger and the fun begins. As a single, you're going to learn to partner-up in an entirely different way. And, no matter which people you select to be on your Dream Team, know that you are better equipped for success when you have the right people in your inner circle of career support to offer advice and keep you going.

Setting up Your Dream Team

Partner up in a new way. Sometimes it isn't easy being that "horse of a different color" in your group of friends. If everyone you know is consumed with corporate jobs, but you have a strong urge to strike out on your own, you may get resistance from those who can't relate to your dream or are concerned you are making a mistake.

The solution is not to try to persuade the naysayers. Instead, seek like-minded people to share your experiences with. It's so important to feel like you have someone who understands what you're going through during the sometimes unpredictable yet exhilarating career transition time.

Identify at least one person to help hold you accountable. You can also pair up on projects with someone already established in your field. It will be an excellent learning experience and you'll have a checks-and-balances system in place.

Take a few moments now to think about where you can find a partner to support you during this process—a friend, family member, maybe even a co-worker. Write the names of these people in your Career Journal. Brainstorm, narrow those new ideas down, and then *ask the partner you've chosen for what you need*.

Speak up. What do you need most to make this transition happen? What kind of support will you require?

Ask for it. Be prepared for people to not only listen, but to have several ideas on how you might get to where you want to be. Be courageous in your asking. Think how empowered you'll feel when you have accomplished even more than you thought possible with the help of a few trusted confidantes.

Hang around with people you want to be like. To borrow a quote from life coach Victoria Moran: *"Surround yourself with positivity. Feed your spirit with the company of upbeat, 'land-on-their-feet' friends."* When you proactively choose people who boost your energy and make you feel good, you can't help but improve your motivation. Like attracts like. It's a simple concept and easy to apply.

You already know how it feels when you spend time with someone whose outlook on life is negative; it tends to bring you down. Being around optimistic people gives you an instant mood lift and an infusion of positive energy, an especially good thing on those days you may not be feeling so upbeat. Take a moment to look at the people in your life—those you work with, as well as your family and friends. Who supports you for who you are as a person? Who makes you feel good about yourself and your life? Whom do you admire? Make it a point to spend time with these people more often. Absorb their positive vibrations.

You also can find career-seeking buddies by visiting online and in-person networks where career seekers converge. Take a career education course or career teleclass. Reach out to classmates, or ask your career coach to introduce you to others in their circle of contacts.

Have your mentor on your dream team. If you've identified a mentor, make sure you continue to cultivate and nurture that relationship. Adding your mentor to your dream team as someone who has been where you are headed can be extremely valuable as you move forward in your transition. Is there someone in your life you admire because they didn't follow the status quo? Someone who made their own way or just seems to be living out an amazingly full and satisfying life and career? Maybe you have a friend, relative, or acquaintance who started their own business or managed to weave creativity and flexibility into their professional life in a way that stands out from the crowd.

Now is a perfect time to ask for advice and guidance from your mentor(s) and to keep in touch by adding them to your dream team. Listen to their stories, learn from their mistakes, and apply this knowledge to the changes you're experiencing in your own career. Be sure you acknowledge how much you appreciate their time and energy. Treat them to lunch, but don't take so much of their time that you're leaning on them too much. Be respectful of their time and take your cues from them about how much time and energy they can give you.

Try individual career coaching or counseling. I offer what is known as Co-Active Coaching—a style of coaching that empowers career seekers to find the right answers on their own, to navigate their career course in a way that feels right for them alone. A good coach will never merely hand you a set of instructions. You can expect an objective viewpoint, expert advice, and positive encouragement. The suggestions offered should be individually customized to help you manage your unique, specific goals effectively in a manner that works for you.

When looking for and working with a career coach, be prepared to identify what you most need help with, to state your goals with as much specificity as you can, and be clear about what you want and expect to get out of the coaching relationship.

It's understandable that our human support group won't always exist in the places we're accustomed to having it, but help is out there. Whether you choose coaching, counseling, mentorship, support groups, or a combination of all of these, have confidence that you will find and receive the guidance and understanding you need to move forward with your dream of the ultimate career for you.

Quick Tip Reinforcement: Share Selectively

We've discussed this, but it bears repeating. Remember to share your dream or plans only with those whom you know will be supportive. Given what we've already covered, this may seem obvious but it's easy to forget. In the excitement of moving forward, you may forget that some people in your life tend to be negative by pointing out why you shouldn't do something or why you can't expect to achieve your career dream. Sometimes holding back on sharing until you're really rock solid in your dream is the best way to proceed.

Of course, share your dream with your Dream Team MVPs, but don't waste precious time with people who make you feel as if you have to defend your dream.

Feel Better Now. It's important to feel better *now*, in the present, while you're looking ahead toward your new career path or job. If you are feeling intensely miserable, so out of balance, unfulfilled, frustrated in your life or in your current work position, it will be harder to dream and focus on the future. Sometimes the quickest fix for feeling better "in the now" is a little inspiration.

Consider these inspirational accounts:

- Babe Ruth is remembered as the "Home Run King." He was also the "Strike-Out Champion," having failed at bat 1,330 times, more than any other player in the major leagues at that time.
- The head of a drama school in 1927 advised Lucille Ball to try another profession because she would never make it as an actress. She went on to have a history-making television series and eventually owned her own movie and television studio.
- In 1962, an executive of Decca Records made the following statement about a singing group: "We don't like their sound. Besides, groups playing guitars are on the way out anyway." He was talking about the Beatles.
- A corporate buyout of Handy Dan Home Improvement Centers forced two executives to lose their jobs in 1978. A year later, Arthur Blank and Bernard Marcus joined another co-worker, Ronald Brill, to

start their own do-it-yourself home improvement warehouse store called Home Depot, now North America's largest home improvement retailer.

- Emmeline Snively, director of the Blue Book Modeling Agency, told modeling hopeful Norma Jean Baker in 1944, "You'd better learn secretarial work or else get married." She went on to become Marilyn Monroe.

Feeling better? Take a moment now to look at your dream again. This time just list the high points in your Career Journal—the accomplishments that really shine in your dream. Write rapidly, don't censor yourself in any way. Just let the thoughts flow freely—positive words, phrases, whatever comes to mind. Then focus on to those high points throughout your day to feel even better.

7

Pulling Out All the Stops
Conquering What Prevents You from Moving Forward

We've talked about many ways to make your transition as smooth and successful as possible by getting support, managing your finances, Dreaming First and dreaming BIG. As you continue to move forward, you may experience what many of my clients have experienced as they initially embarked on their transitions. See if this fits:

You're still a bit nervous about making the change, but you feel enthusiastic and pumped up about the future. You're positive and highly focused. But as time goes on, a few obstacles crop up, just as they do in any other area of your life. Roadblocks between you and your dream career. Here are some ways you can maneuver around them with more ease.

Roadblock 1: **Do I Take the "Bennies" or Do I Jet?
How To Really Know What's Best.**

Here's a common scenario:

> The salary and benefits and other perks of my job
> are so good that I feel like I should stay. My family
> and friends think I'd be crazy to leave a package
> deal like the one offered with my position. I'm at a
> loss for what to do.

While great benefits and money are a big draw now, remember to keep the whole, larger picture at the forefront
of your mind—your future career perspective. And, if you
are stuck in the "I should stay where I am, I'd be crazy to
leave" mentality then ask yourself these questions:

- Do I feel stimulated and challenged each day?
- Is the work inspiring? Does it feel like I'm doing
  what I'm meant to do?
- Is the position in line with the career direction I'd
  like to head?
- How much potential for growth is left in my current
  job? Is there room to move up the ladder and learn
  new marketable skills? Or, have I hit the glass ceiling at this particular company?
- What is the current state of the market where I'm
  employed? Is there a danger that if I hang around
  for too long, I could wake up without a job one day

and find myself under-qualified for the next opportunity that comes along?

Many companies entice their employees with juicy benefit
packages, generous vacation plans, and other incentives.
But if the job isn't a fit for you, it's not a fit regardless of the
perks. And, if the job offers no room for advancement, all
you'll succeed in doing by staying is delaying your career
growth.

Roadblock 2: **Too Many Choices.**

Here's the scenario:

> There are so many options. I don't know which
> way to turn. Certain aspects of the job I have now
> make me want to stay, while others have me eyeing
> the door. I have several ideas about 'what I'd like
> to do when I grow up,' but some areas of my skill
> set seem too underdeveloped to branch out on my
> own. I'm at different stages in a few different tal-
> ent areas. I feel overwhelmed and unable to make
> a decision about any aspect of my career.

If you feel overwhelmed, just getting a sense that something
needs to change is an important awareness. It is better to
recognize that there is a problem, and experience confusion
about how to solve it, than to fail to realize that something
is missing at all and stagnate in one spot.

Gaining clarity is an ongoing process. More self-exploration and greater flexibility are usually needed. You've already identified many aspects of your dream. Now is a good time to redefine that new, fulfilling and rewarding career path *before* you jump into another job that might not be a fit for you. Consider investing in yourself more specifically, targeting your efforts on gaining greater clarity. You can sign up for a career exploration class or take a career test. Be sure to give yourself the space and breathing room to really figure this out. You'll be glad you did.

Roadblock 3: **Family Members Don't Understand.**

Here's the scenario:

> Ever since my parents found out I was thinking about quitting my job, they have nothing but disapproving looks, defeatist remarks, and general pessimism toward my endeavor. As I edge ever closer to making my job transition complete, I feel that I am in need of more and more support but I have less and less encouragement from mom and dad. How do I get around that and still survive all these changes?

It's not uncommon for parents, or other family members of their generation, to take a conservative stance on the topic of your career. In generations past, if workers stayed loyal to one company, they were assured that they would be "taken care of." Advancement, regular pay raises, and a generous retirement package were expected. Today, with so many mergers and market shifts, staying loyal to one company is not enough to ensure a secure future. It's difficult to explain this to parents or other family members who enjoyed this sense of security throughout their working years. They came into their own during an entirely different era.

If it upsets you to talk to your parents about your career transition, don't do it right away. Wait until a time when you feel more sure of yourself and you can offer your parents information that will reassure them that things are going well for you, or you can do it as soon as you are bringing in a decent wage and are able to support yourself.

It would be nice if we could always rely on our parents to be understanding of our emotional needs, but life doesn't always iron out without a few wrinkles. You can, and will, find other ways to find support.

More Ways To Cope with Family

- Have an honest conversation with your parents. Tell them what makes you happy and that you need their love and support at this exciting, yet sometimes scary, time in your life.
- Get a sense of when it's okay to share your news and when it's probably better to hold back. You will get better at this as you grow into the changes and begin to get a taste of real success.
- If you need a parent figure to reassure you during those unsteady first stages of career change, seek out a good friend who has been there. Caring friends, coaches and peers can ease the stress during times of crisis or need.

Little do your parents know how absolutely thrilled and proud of you they are going to feel when you finally tell them the wonderful news of your success. I know because I myself have been there. My parents were worried about me, and now are absolutely thrilled that I am doing something I love.

Roadblock 4: **Under Pressure.**

The scenario:

> Since I'm the 'only one' I must make the right career choice, and that puts too much pressure on me. If I try to outline a series of goals, there are too many areas where I don't know the answers yet because I haven't gotten that far. Having a plan that's missing certain details really freaks me out. I won't make a move because the move has to be perfect.

As we've discussed earlier, although many career seekers feel uncomfortable when there are pieces missing from the puzzle, there will never be a perfect moment when it's 100% safe to take action. That said, it should be your goal to take small steps toward what you want. Ease into your job transition gradually. Take it slow, at a pace that's comfortable for you—one step at a time. Work small changes into your current schedule, and as you grow more confident, allow the changes to become more substantial. Even something as simple as reading this career seekers book counts as a step. You can manage the risks and assess what you learn in small increments along the way.

You can still shoot for the stars and listen to your intuition about what is a fit for you, but small baby steps will get you there more comfortably. You'll find it will still be an adventure, just a much more pleasurable, relaxing one.

As I said before, just keep stepping and you will eventually get where you want to be.

Roadblock 5: I'm Not Finding Support from My Friends.

The scenario:

> Sometimes when I try to talk about my career move with friends, I get blank stares. Or they try to give me well-meaning advice that doesn't fit or won't work for me.

We've touched on family members and friends who may not understand, and now we're going to talk a bit more about your friends. If you're going about this the right way, along with your new set of career responsibilities you will have found a new set of pals to relate to on a professional level: Your Dream Team. Don't worry about other friends who may not be able to support you in the way you need to be supported at this time. You are not losing your old pals. During the implementation phase of your transition, if you notice certain friends trigger those negative voices in your head, steer clear of the career transition topic when you're with them. Focus on other things so that you can still spend time together, without having your negative voices activated.

View it as having different friends for different purposes. You have those friends you always go to for relationship advice, the friends who can relate to your frustrations with your family, and the friends who you enjoy on a night out. To that list you have now added a set of career buddies. These Dream Team friends will be your best source of moral support in the professional sense, so take good care in cultivating such relationships. You aren't losing your old friends, you're just expanding your reach to meet your new career needs. You will be so glad to have both the new and the old friendships in your life.

Ways to Nourish Your Whole Self

As you continue to overcome obstacles and create new opportunities, be sure to take time to nourish yourself—your personal self. Sometimes we're so busy taking care of business that we forget to take care of ourselves. Yet, if you're in the midst of a major career change, there is nothing more important than listening to your inner voice and tending to all the little things your body, mind, and soul needs to stay balanced.

Exercise your body while you expand your mind. So many of us spend the majority of our days sitting in front of a computer, both at our jobs and at home. It's no wonder that insomnia and being overweight have reached epidemic proportions for millions of Americans. As always, but especially at a time of career change when stress levels are higher, regular exercise is vital to your well-being. Make it a priority to engage in some kind of aerobic exercise at least three times a week. Pilates, Tae-Bo, and yoga are all excellent ways to reduce tension, properly align the body, and keep energy flow on an even keel.

No matter which type of exercise you choose, you can use this time to work on the more pressing issues in your career and the changes you are making. Think about it: how many times have you sat in front of the television not hearing or seeing a thing because you're consumed with what's happening in your life? Taking time out to reduce your stress level by exercising, while focusing on your goals, stumbling blocks, or major decisions, will ease your body and mind and help you feel good both mentally and physically. Some of my best ideas have come to me when I'm out exercising and thinking outside the box.

There are so many things you can do to keep your mind, body, and spirit functioning at peak performance during this exciting time of change. Remember that, even though your current focus is on your career and how to best navigate the transition, you are still a human being. You deserve a balanced life of learning, new experiences, solitary time, social activities, and spiritual growth. Remember to give yourself these gifts and you will feel whole, at peace, and ready for whatever comes your way. And don't forget to have fun. Often we leave that out of the equation when enjoying ourselves along the journey is the best part of all.

Review your transition progress regularly. You're already keeping a Career Journal, but making a point to review it regularly will boost your spirits and help you maintain a healthy perspective.

Devote at least one night per week to writing down your thoughts about your transition, recording milestones in the process, and letting go of emotions by putting pen to paper. Of course, you don't have to limit your journal entries to once a week. Write in your Career Journal whenever you feel inspired, even if it's every night. When you go back and read your previous journal entries to remind yourself of where you're going and where you've been, you will be pleasantly surprised at the progress you've made. You can also create an online blog in which you invite other career seekers to ponder your musings and offer their opinions or stories.

Set Your Boundaries

Life can get a little crazy when change is happening all around us. If you've still got one foot in your current professional role and the other foot is stepping into the future, you may feel unsure of whether you're coming or going. This is a natural feeling in transition. The trick is to set boundaries for yourself to curb feelings of being overwhelmed.

One boundary could be managing some of the channels of information overflow. For example, if you've signed up for career-related e-mail newsletters, you can create a special e-mail address for this purpose alone. This way, personal pursuits can be kept separate from your daily responsibilities, helping you to feel less distracted and stressed.

Time can be another boundary that keeps anxiety at bay. For instance, you can make a commitment not to think about anything career-related after 8:00 p.m. Instead, reserve another time slot for this purpose. Your commitment could be, "I will work on my career transition from 5:30-7:30 p.m. at least twice a week." By setting and maintaining boundaries between your career goals, everyday responsibilities, and leisure activities, you will feel more in control of your life, as well as more balanced and at peace with yourself and the process.

• • • • •

Learn to Manage Your Disempowering Beliefs

We all have them. Those of us who are single can have disempowering beliefs specific to our situation, ones that continue to repeat: We can't make a change because we're alone and it's only us. We have only ourselves to rely on. While it's true that you are on your own, this doesn't mean you can't make a successful career change. You just might have to do it a little differently. And that's okay. You *can* make a plan and make it happen.

Identify any disempowering beliefs you may have about making this transition as a single person. For instance, thinking that you can't do it or that it's harder as a single person. Create new, empowering, positive beliefs that become your mantra for success. For example, *Other singles have successfully made a transition, I can too.* Use the Self Reflection

Strengthening Exercise to help you create more empowering beliefs and greater focus on positive thoughts.

Take these words of Marianne Williamson to heart:

*Our deepest fear is not that we are inadequate. It is that we are
powerful beyond measure. Our light, not our darkness, most
frightens us. We ask ourselves, 'Who am I to be brilliant, gor-
geous, and talented?' Actually, who are you not to be?*

Exercise: Self-Reflection Strengthening to Boost Your Success Quotient

Write down your answers to these statements:

1. The great things about me are:

2. I've already come so far in my career and I want to
    keep going. Here's a recap of what I have done and
    why I am proud of myself:

3. I am never alone. The people who can give me strength
    and support during my career transition are:

4. If I have a problem, I know that there is always
    more than one way of looking at things and arriv-
    ing at a solution. The last big challenge I made it
    through was:

5. I know that (job title) is perfect for me because my talents are (list them):

6. Next time I work on my career, I plan to add one more action to the list (could be a simple phone call or quick piece of additional research):

In the following chapter you'll find more answers from singles who have successfully made a career transition and are thrilled they made the move! They are success stories from some of my clients who identified their ideal career path and made it happen. These clients were willing to share their ups and downs with you so you can become your own success story. Each client reveals what tips they used the most, and most importantly, why they used them.

8

Making It Happen
Success Stories from Singles in Transition

These success stories are from a few of my career coaching clients—individuals at varying stages of career transition. I hope their stories inspire and encourage you to continue on your path toward your dream career. Look for valuable lessons that you can apply in your own life. Here's to your continued success in transitioning to your dream career!

Achieving the Best of Both Worlds

Tara Scarlett

Tara Scarlett knows that dream careers do not always fit in a box, nor do they always match the prescribed nine-to-five mold. When she decided to leave her position with a marketing agency, some of her family and friends thought she was crazy. They wondered why she would want to leave a job she was good at and paid well. But Tara had bigger dreams so she boldly ventured out on her own to pursue her dream of being a professional photographer.

To her surprise, she soon discovered that she loved the stability of the corporate world *and* the freedom of owning her own business. So she decided to do both. Tara found a market research position she loves and that pays her bills while she continues to pursue her passion for photography. She found a way to break the mold and have the best of both worlds. Here's how Tara turned a dream into an ongoing success story.

Q. What steps did you take to make this happen?
The first thing I had to do was develop a financial plan to take care of my bills. I also asked for support from my friends and family, but what has helped me the most is having a career coach—a supportive person who is objective and probing, someone who helps me listen to myself, set a plan, and remain focused. Reading has also helped me. There are a lot of great stories out there about people who have made changes to follow their passions. After uncovering my dream, I took inspiration from these stories and from my coach. I focused on getting the courage to move forward with my dream, and then I just went for it. I am single with a mortgage and bills to consider. I have no other source of income and no relationship support. I have me. I provide my own financial and emotional support, and I am following my dream!

Q. What challenges did you encounter and how did you handle them?

My greatest challenge has been deciding which direction I want to take and knowing that I have to do it on my own. I have focused on myself and what will make me, not others, happy.

Q. Were there naysayers? How did you manage to stay the course?

Yes, there have been naysayers—myself included. My internal gremlins (negative voices) were the worst of all. I've been reading and working with my coach on how to manage those disempowering beliefs. I have had to focus a lot on controlling my pessimistic inner critic. Outside naysayers, including family and friends, say things without understanding where I am coming from or make comments with their own agendas in mind. I learned to stop discussing my passions with others until I was able to speak with confidence about my decision. This decision is not about anyone else. It is about me, my happiness, my choices, and my future.

Q. What words of wisdom would you share with others?

You never know what you can accomplish unless you try. For me, I won't look back one day and regret not trying. There is a quote from an unknown author that I like: 'Years from now you will be more disappointed by the things that you didn't do than by the ones you did do. So throw off the bowlines. Sail away from the safe harbor. Catch the trade winds in your sails. Explore. Dream. Discover.'

Q. What's the best part of your experience?
I love my work! That is the best thing about my career transition. The process of learning that I could give myself permission to let go of the old and start something new— that was the hardest part and also the most rewarding.

Tips from Tara's Story

- Develop a financial plan to take care of your bills.
- Ask for financial, mental, and emotional support from friends and family.
- Get support from a coach or mentor.
- Work on managing your disempowering beliefs so they do not hold you back.
- Focus on what will make you, not others, happy.

• • • • •

The Journey of Self Discovery

Wendy McGee

Wendy McGee worked in marketing for more than two decades before admitting she was unhappy with her career path. She no longer had any enthusiasm for her work. Wendy wanted her career to be more than eight draining hours of managing accounts, projects, and strategy development for an ad agency.

As she gained the courage to explore other career opportunities, she learned a lot about herself, her goals, and her dreams along the way. She is now in the process of growing her dream of empowering children and enhancing their learning.

Q. What career path were you on, and what made you decide to change?
Before I started on this journey, I had been in marketing in one form or another for over 20 years. My last marketing job was at an advertising and marketing agency in Atlanta. I worked on the business side of the agency, managing accounts, projects, strategy development, etc. It was a job I was good at doing but it had lost its appeal and became just a demanding job. I wasn't miserable, but I wasn't happy either. I felt like there had to be more. Then, as often happens in agencies, several contracts were lost, and I became a victim of downsizing. It was a blow, but, at the same time, part of me was relieved.

Q. What steps did you take to move forward?
I knew I needed to take the time to figure out next steps toward a new direction. What I found was that, while I knew myself and the things that I thought would make me happy, it was overwhelming to dig through it all. That is when I found a coach to help me ask the questions that needed to be asked and hold me accountable each week for taking action.

Q. What have you discovered about yourself through this process?
What struck me during the process and really spurred me to make some big changes was when I compared the values

and priorities that I had been living by for the previous three months and the ideal values and priorities I wanted to live by—they were polar opposites. That was a surprise to me and a wake-up call.

I have also had the opportunity to catch my breath, and new thoughts and realizations have come to me that have caused me to realize that the thing I want to do most is work with children.

Q. How have you worked toward identifying your dream? What steps are you taking to make this happen?
The process hasn't been a straight path. I have explored several career options (starting a training company that got as far as research before I realized that it wasn't the path for me) and have tried another job (HR-related) believing that would be an avenue that would fit. I have also worked on a children's book. For me, I seem to make the most progress when I have the time to analyze what I have done, not pen to paper type of analysis, but realizing how it makes me feel and how my energy around it felt. That has helped guide me.

Q. What has been your biggest obstacle?
When you are responsible for supporting yourself, the pressure is on to figure things out quickly. Sometimes I can scare myself silly by getting into disaster mode. I worry that I am wasting time or that I can't figure this out. I get tired of the transition. In fact, sometimes I am just exhausted from trying to figure things out. To break this cycle I will read a favorite book, take a walk, sit on the porch and look at the beautiful trees, and visit friends. I know if I

quit, I would regret it and sometimes that is the only thing that keeps me moving forward when I am really thinking I have done something crazy by leaving the life I had. When things really get to me, either fear or frustration or exhaustion, I get moving. Sometimes I clean. Sometimes I go for a speed walk—just something physical to get me out of my head and get me thinking in a different way.

Q. What unique issues do you think single people face?
When you are self-supporting, how you are going to pay bills is always in the back of your mind. I have always been a saver, and I was fortunate to have savings. However, it is still scary to think about what you are going to do and how you are going to accomplish it. The transition period has taken longer than I expected, and if I didn't have some cushion, I would not have been able to stick with this excursion into the unknown. I think that I am much more cautious than if I had the support of a spouse—even if it was just moral support. Some of that is my personality, but I think that it is a common desire to have a sense of security. I have found it to be more difficult to really "go for it with abandon" because I want to make sure that I have a plan for taking care of myself.

Q. Where is your path leading you?
I am close to landing a day job that will, I believe, provide me with some stability while allowing me to work on my career path on the side. I will have the energy at the end of the day to put into the things that are important to me. I am working toward finding a career that will revolve

around nurturing and empowering children through non-traditional learning techniques. I am excited about what the future holds!

Q. What words of wisdom would you share?
Understand that this isn't a straight shot. The path has many turns and twists and is full of many grace notes. I am very glad I did this; it has been full of discovery and is really a confidence booster in many ways. It is taking theory and turning it into reality and even though it is not as planned, it is much richer than imagined. Find the things that give you comfort and use them when things are challenging. Find a support group. It is invaluable. A career coach is helpful too. Having someone to hold you accountable, be a good cheerleader, and give you positive energy is a real boost.

Tips from Wendy's Story

- Realize this is a process, and it may not be a linear path. There may be twists and turns along the way to making your dream career happen. Be flexible.
- Find support and someone to hold you accountable and give you encouragement.
- Have a plan for taking care of yourself financially, emotionally and mentally.
- Manage your thoughts and emotions when you become frustrated, anxious or fearful. Do something you love to get out of the funk.

• • • • •

Leading By Example

. . . .

Karin C. Smith

At the age of 40, Karin C. Smith came to the realization that her career path choices had never been strategic or planned. As a result, her directionless career seemed to be lacking purpose and fulfillment. Karin decided to take charge of her career and move forward with intentionality. She recently started her own business in affiliation with an international company, and her career has become an opportunity for her to live out her values, passions, and aspirations.

Q. What made you decide to change your career path?
I realized that most of my career decisions in the past had been made in a vacuum. Although I could find a common thread in my diverse work experiences, there was a haphazardness to my work and life choices. Through career coaching, I sought to synthesize my breadth and depth of work experience into an integrated and self-sustaining whole.

Q. What have you discovered about yourself?
I have learned that finding my ideal career path is about stepping wholly into being a leader and role model in every area of my life. I now pursue leadership as a way of life, rather than as a role in the workplace so that there are many ways that my leadership is expressed. My career/life path is about developing courage in myself and in others. I am now able to recognize, articulate, and achieve my dreams. I have also learned that career development is a

process, like everything else in life. The journey is really more important than the outcome.

Q. What challenges have been most difficult?
Often times, I've felt that honoring my values, purpose, and passion in the workplace has been detrimental to my career success. At times, I've felt misunderstood. Ultimately, these difficult situations have helped me to define my path. I have learned that leadership is about facing challenges and growing with them. Through coaching and the loving encouragement and support of my family and many dear friends, I have stepped into this wisdom.

Also, for much of my career I've accepted "scraping by" and living "check-to-check" as an acceptable reality. Through coaching, I've been working to change this mentality and to attract all the material and financial resources I need to live a balanced life.

Q. What excited you most about your career transition?
There have been times when I've felt particularly savvy in my career and this can be very exciting. I once increased my salary by 43% when I left one job and moved to another. This happened because I had learned it was important to negotiate for my salary rather than taking what was offered. I had the support of my coach as I took that risk.

I am also ecstatic that I finally started the executive MBA program at Loyola College in Maryland. This was a goal I identified when I was being trained as a coach. Going to graduate school is by far one of the best decisions I've made for my career. My fellow students, the team environment, the rigorous academics, the challenge of juggling a career and my studies—it's been very rewarding both personally and professionally.

Q. How do you view your career path today?
Being single, I've had great flexibility in life and career because I've had the freedom to make my own choices. Because I am single and do not have dependent children, I've been able to take more financial risks . . . too many, at times.

I've had a very unique and wonderful work experience . . . not always financially lucrative . . . but truly abundant in so many ways. I would not trade my path because it has been my best teacher. The work now is about receiving long-term abundance, achieving mastery, being of service and, most important, having fun!

Tips from Karin's Story

- Career development is a process, like everything else in life. The journey is really more important than the outcome.
- Being single, you have great flexibility in life and in your career because you have the freedom to make your own choices.
- Enjoy the process, it can be your best teacher.

• • • • •

The Freedom To Change

. . . .

Julianne Manske

Julianne Manske knew what she loved to do—connect with people—but she didn't know what career would offer her the most opportunity to do this. Julianne worked at several different jobs before realizing that she needed to make a major career change if she were ever going to find a truly fulfilling career. In the end, she found her ultimate career path in helping others find their dream careers.

Q. What made you decide to make a major career change?
After graduating with an English degree, I followed my interest in the media to a media planning job at Starcom in Chicago. The job provided me with an excellent overview of the different media outlets and how they are bought and sold. However, my position involved too many numbers and not enough creativity, writing and idea generation.

My fascination with the media led me to Los Angeles to pursue my dream of becoming an entertainment publicist. The work was difficult, but the job had a lot of elements of glitz and glamour. However, there was still something missing, and I couldn't figure out exactly what it was.

Q. How have you worked toward identifying your dream career?
I had to ask myself, "What is it about the media that is attractive to me?" I decided that it was the element of story, of learning about people's lives and the ideas, trends, and

happenings of our society. At the beginning of this year, I started training to be a career coach myself, because I realized that the piece I liked most of all of my past jobs was connecting with people and finding out what makes them tick. Career coaching achieves that connection on a very deep, fulfilling level.

Q. What steps did you take to make this happen?
As I began working with Hallie as my career coach, she was able to point out my 'gremlins,' and the things I would say that were actually coming from other people in my life, or from my own subconscious—things like, 'You need to make money,' and 'What makes you think you'd be good at that?' Career coaching was key in sorting through those voices to find my own voice and discovering my dream career.

Q. What obstacles have you faced?
I myself was the biggest obstacle on my road to deciding to pursue a career in coaching. I struggled with self-doubt and internal dialogue that told me coaching isn't secure enough, that I can't make money doing it, and that I'm not going to be good at it.

Q. How have you moved through these roadblocks?
Visioning, imagining my future, is what helped give me the courage and incentive to push through any blocks. When I picture my ideal self—the person I will become five, ten, twenty years from now—I realize what I need to do today to position myself to reach my highest vision for myself.

Q. What unique challenges do you think singles face?
In terms of challenges, as a single person, I feel that my
friends and family support my career transitions. But that's
not the same as a husband creating a life vision with me, or
supporting me so I can take chances, or being there whether or not my risks pay off. Also, as a single person, I have
to support myself financially when I am between jobs or
looking for something more fulfilling.

Q. What advantages do you think single people have?
I think that being single has definite advantages and disad-
vantages in terms of career transitions. The biggest advantage for me was the freedom to pick up and move across the
country without having to consider a boyfriend or husband
when making that decision.

Q. What was the peak moment of your transition?
This is a tough question because there was so much about
making the decision to become a coach that was exciting.
The first thing that comes to mind is actually taking the
first step and committing the time and money to my training. That was a proud moment for me because I felt that my
actions and commitments were completely aligned with my
skills, gifts and values. That was the first time I'd felt that
direct of a connection to my career path. Also, not everyone
in my life understood coaching or saw it as a valuable or
lucrative career, and it was powerful to stand strong in my
career decision despite these opinions. So the first weekend
of coach training, when I started to see myself as a coach,
was a very proud moment. I really connected with the ma-

terials in training, and completely lit up whenever I talked about coaching. I was so proud and knew that I had made the right decision. So, as I said, this is a tough question. Lots of parts of the process for me were exciting!

Tips from Julianne's Story

- Sort through the negative voices to find your own.
- Visioning and imagining your future, can help you find the courage and incentive to push through any blocks.
- Learn to overcome self doubt.

• • • • •

Blessings In Disguise

Anna Vacca

Anna Vacca was laid off from her job at a trucking company. She was scared and didn't know what to do next, but somehow she just knew that being laid off was the best thing that could've happened to her. It was time to find her passion and pursue something she truly enjoyed.

Through our work together, Anna realized that being a loan processor was her dream job. She would be able to help people purchase and finance their first homes. Her way with people, outgoing personality, and her desire to help others made this a perfect match. As if by divine intervention, Anna met a woman who was willing to be her mentor in this field. She gave Anna a job, and is now helping her develop her new career path. Here are lessons you can learn from her experience:

Q. How did you react when you were laid off?
I was working in a job I couldn't stand until I was lucky enough to get laid off. What to do? I didn't have a clue. I just knew I didn't want to go back. I knew I had to find the silver lining of the situation. I soon realized that being laid off was one of the best things that has happened to me.

Q. What challenges did you encounter along the way, and how did you handle them?
I had to realize that I would be okay and that I would be able to find another job. I had to find the courage inside myself to create a new path and not just jump into another unfulfilling job. It takes courage to admit you're unhappy and decide to take steps toward fixing it, but you have to realize that this is your life. If you are unhappy, find the courage to do something about it.

Q. What is the first step you took toward finding a new career?
It was overwhelming and hard to find a place to start. I'd never really had the time to even think about what I would really enjoy doing. Then another thought came to mind, "What would I enjoy doing AND get paid enough to actually do it?" So I read everything I could to figure it out and really do something to help myself during such a confusing time.

Q. What words of wisdom would you share with others who are taking steps to create their own paths?
Take action toward your dream career. Even small steps are better than standing still. When in doubt, just take the next small step.

Q. What transition experiences were most memorable?
The peak experience for me was finally having a clearer picture in mind of what I wanted and finally learning who I was! In the coaching class with you, there were a few very important things I needed to do before I could even think about another job direction. Figuring out my values was something I had never done before. It really helped me realize what environment was a fit for me. Thinking about my future self really helped me see who I wanted to be, and I think I pulled some parts of me out that I was holding in deep inside. I wouldn't have been able to do anything if I couldn't get past the 'gremlins' that had been building up my entire life. All of this helps with more self confidence overall.

After getting involved with something I had finally figured out I wanted at the time, which was working as a loan officer, another opportunity came up that was truly my dream job. The opportunity came up to move to South Korea and teach English, which opened up the door to live in another country and travel all over the world! I'm currently living out my childhood dreams.

This situation gave me the awareness that even when you're down, things can change drastically and before you know it, everything can change for the better . . . if you really want it. It seemed like once I transformed my thinking I started to attract everything I wanted. Thanks Hallie for the opportunity to share my story. It's exciting to look back at the transition. It's crazy to think back to where I was just one year ago at this time.

Tips from Anna's Story

- See the silver lining. When something negative happens to you, ask yourself—what's the possible silver lining in this situation?
- Have courage to admit you are unhappy and do something about it.
- Invest in yourself. Take the time to define your ideal career.
- Take action toward your dream career, even if they are small steps. Don't stand still.

Bonus Section #1
Creating a Killer Resume

You've probably read a lot about writing your resume and the best way to capture a prospective employer's attention. Here are the best tips and ideas I have seen. Review them before you start working on your resume.

Tip 1: Before Diving Right In, Make a Plan First.

. . . .

If you're anything like me, you may want to just dive right in and start writing or revising your resume immediately. Hold on for a moment. I know how you feel because this is how I used to do things, but take a step back and answer the following questions first:

- What do I want to accomplish with this resume?
- For which specific job is this resume? Remember, you want to adjust the content and potentially the layout of your resume to each job you apply for as

needed. This is an obvious tip most people know, but in the heat of sending out resumes it can be easy to forget.

- Read the advertisement for the job again. Put yourself in the employer's shoes: What do they need to know about me in order to make a decision about whether to call me for an interview? What is most important to them in a potential employee, what are they looking for? Based on the job description, what skills, experience and talents do I need to highlight? Then, be sure to include these items in your resume—front and center.

Keep in mind, you need to let them know exactly why you are a better choice than the next job candidate who comes along. That means offering tangible evidence of your value. When you think of something positive to include on your list of career accomplishments, figure out a way to position your statement about that accomplishment so that it appeals to the reader from a standpoint of need.

Finally, make a full list of your natural talents and abilities, as well as your accomplishments. Brainstorm what your natural talents and abilities are. Write down everything you've accomplished in your life. This will not only help you get everything out there on paper as items to possibly include in your resume, but it will boost your confidence as well.

Tip 2: Give Yourself Credit. Don't Discount What Comes Naturally to You.

Have you noticed that people tend to downplay the things they are naturally good at? This is very typical; I've done it myself. This is because we assume that when something comes naturally to us, everyone must be good at it, right? Wrong.

Just because you can easily organize your office or keep your files in amazing working order doesn't mean that comes naturally to everyone. It doesn't. So give yourself credit. In what areas do you excel that others don't?

Tip 3: Talk to Those Who Know You Well.

If you're still not sure what you are naturally good at, ask others—family members, friends, former coworkers. This is a great tool for identifying your natural talents and abilities. Ask them questions like: What makes me stand out? What am I naturally good at that sticks in your mind? How have I helped you in the past with a problem, issue, or challenge you were having?

Tip 4: Organize Your Resume in a Way Best for the Job.

As a career coach, one of the things people frequently ask me is, "Do I have to put my resume in chronological order?"

The answer is no, you don't. This is especially relevant if you are changing career fields. In this case, chronological order isn't necessary; relevance is more important because you're making a leap to another field. If you prefer date order, and it seems particularly appropriate for the job you're hunting for, go for it. But I typically recommend highlighting your skills and accomplishments that are relevant to the position and organizing your resume accordingly. Place the most relevant jobs at the top. If you have a spotty job record, this helps minimize the issue.

Tip 5: Keep It Concise and Easy To Read.

Enough said. You don't want to send a potential employer a novel, and you want the hiring manager to be able to read and scan your resume with ease. Keep it short and sweet while highlighting why you're the best for the job.

Tip 6: Stress Contributions, Not Duties.

Resumes should always highlight what you contributed or accomplished at a job, as opposed to duties or responsibilities. This is another area I notice people tend to struggle. They want to list their job description. Don't do this. Instead, tell them how you contributed to that organization. Use action verbs and highlight those accomplishments relevant to the position for which you're applying.

Think of your career resume as your personal selling tool. Remember, your purpose in creating it is to persuade the reader that you're the perfect person for the job.

Tip 7: Get Professional Help.

Yes, many of you may believe you can revise or write your resume yourself and do a decent job. You probably can, and you may even do a great job. I've done this myself. However, when I see a resume written by a professional resume writer, I notice the difference immediately. After you've completed the preliminary preparation tips (1 through 6), I highly recommend getting professional help if your budget allows.

When I need something that I know is not my specialty, I ask the experts. The professionals know what they're doing and can help you develop a winning resume that gets you in the door for an interview.

If you need names of top notch resume writers, you can find a list of those I recommend on the Resources Page of my website under Coaching. If you choose not to seek professional help, at the very least get someone to proofread your resume for you. Typos can sometimes be the deciding factor for hiring one person over the next.

Make sure you feel proud of your resume. This will show in the interview. If you're pleased with it, that will come across.

Don't Forget the Cover Letter: Your Cover Letter Checklist

Some of these tips you may have heard before, but it doesn't hurt to look at your cover letter to make sure you've accomplished the following items and checked them off the list.

Use this as your quick checklist for cover letters:

____ 1. **Is it specific and does it demonstrate knowledge?** Employers read many resumes and cover letters. Yours should specifically address the position you hope to land an interview for and explain how your skills and experience qualify you for that job.

____ 2. **Does it effectively play up the positives and explain or downplay the negatives?** Let's say you are a recent college graduate without a lot of job experience. Or you are a single mom who's been out of the workforce for a while. Describe how your activities and experiences in school or during your time off helped prepare you for your career. If you have time gaps in your employment history that you think are necessary to explain, use your cover letter to clarify the gap and put a positive spin on it.

____ 3. **Proofread once more—Is it neat and professional?** It doesn't hurt to proof-read your letter one more time to be safe. As you know, proper punctuation, grammar, and spelling are important in a professional cover letter. Print your resume and cover letter on matching, plain stationery.

Don't miss out on the opportunity the cover letter provides to help you stand out from the crowd of other applicants. A dynamic cover letter will explain what you seek, highlight why you are perfect for the job, and bring personality and voice to your resume.

The Red Flag of Cover Letter Writing

If you're having trouble writing your cover letter and you're not 100% enthusiastic about the job you're applying for, there could be a very good reason. Maybe it's not the ideal job for you after all. Before you finalize your letter, engage in additional exploration to determine whether this is really the perfect career move for you.

Bonus Section #2
Interview Tips for Singles

You've landed a job interview. Congratulations! Now, are you ready? Whether you've been on a dozen interviews (or none), you know your key to success is preparedness.

Be clear about your boundaries. Ask questions about the work environment. You want to make sure you will be able to maintain life balance in your new career. Remember that some employers will assume that as a single person you will be willing and able to work longer hours. If this doesn't work for you, get clear about your boundaries and what you are and aren't willing to do. Are you willing to work late, travel when necessary or pitch in on emergency projects on a regular basis? Find out if these types of things are a requirement of the job so you know what you're getting into.

Don't be reticent during your interview. Ask lots of questions. Remember, you're interviewing them too. You need to be clear about your salary requirement so you will remain financially stable. And, be sure you ask for enough, and ask for what you are worth! Once you get these questions answered to your satisfaction, you are then ready to weigh your options carefully and with greater confidence.

Understand your benefits. Make sure you understand the benefits package and confirm that it covers everything you need. Some employers like to hire contractors instead of full-time employees because they don't have to pay for benefits. Don't make assumptions; as a single you need to know specifically what your benefits are to make sure you are covered. For example, I know some singles choose to go without health insurance or they sacrifice on this part of the package. I don't recommend doing this unless you can find an affordable policy outside of your employer. You also need to know what your disability leave is and termination package just in case your situation changes. I don't suggest focusing on the negative here, but be smart about your choices so that you know you're covered.

Finally, review these general tips for interviewing:

- Relax, you'll be more authentic and confident if you do.
- Be prepared, know the company.
- If they ask about weaknesses or limitations, answer honestly and put a positive spin on it. Explain how you've managed or handled that weakness in order to overcome it.
- Write a list of five key points you plan to express in your interview.
- Write a list of questions, things you need to know.
- Make sure you have the name of the person you'll be interviewing with in advance. If you're uncertain as to the pronunciation of the name, check that too.

- Dress the part. (My mom always says, dress for the job you want, not the job you have!)
- Always wear something that makes you feel confident.

Key Element: How To Interview Your Interviewer

Now it's your turn. When preparing for an interview, most people focus on the questions that might be asked of them and how they will answer. But a key element of a job interview also should be questions you will ask your interviewer.

Why would you interview the interviewer? First, it's as important to you as it is to your potential employer. You need to know if the job is a good fit for your skills, talents and work style. Second, if there is an ideal work situation that you envision for yourself, now is the time to find out if such a position exists, or is likely to be available in the near term. Third, if you were dissatisfied with your last job, you can learn if the situation could be the same in this new place. When the person responsible for hiring has finished giving you the full drill, then go ahead and ask your questions.

Five Key Questions To Ask Your Interviewer

Question 1: Can you describe the work environment?
If possible, find out how many people you'll be reporting to. Ask if you can be introduced to your future boss. Find out

how many people make up the immediate department and in what ways you will be interacting with them. Open up a conversation about the general "scene" of the workplace and the company culture. For example, what is a typical day in the life of someone who holds this position? Ask your interviewer that question too—what is the day like doing the interviewer's job?

Question 2: What types of responsibilities will be expected of me?

Beware of open-ended job titles that could involve numerous duties not detailed in the job description. You might be under the impression that the "marketing coordinator" does things like run and analyze reports, manage advertising campaigns and other sales and marketing projects. Then later on, you discover that your job responsibilities include proofreading and setting up meetings, neither of which you excel at or enjoy. Find out the details before you make a decision.

Question 3: Is there potential for growth?

Many companies have what is known as the "glass ceiling"— few opportunities to advance professionally. You hit a barrier and can't go any higher. The interview is a good time to find out whether the company offers training programs for future leadership positions. Ask if there are openings in areas where you can develop valuable skills. These should be the type of skills you could take with you on the your continuing path of career development. Bear in mind that it's one thing to receive a pay raise every year, quite another if you're forever stuck in the same job with the same duties. If the company has a glass ceiling, it may not be worth making the commitment.

Question 4: Can you tell me about employee benefits, sick day policy, vacations and such?

Save this question for the second interview, assuming there will be one. Some employers find it off-putting when potential job candidates seem overly eager about taking vacation before they're even hired. Nevertheless, these are legitimate, important questions when weighing your options between different potentially rewarding jobs.

Question 5: Will there be travel involved?

To some people, travel is a rewarding aspect of their careers. To others, it's very stressful. Being in an unfamiliar city and managing your time between flights, hotel check-ins, conferences and trade shows can be frenetic. So find out ahead of time how much travel, if any, will be involved and under what circumstances. Do you find travel a stimulating part of doing business? Great. But if you think travel could negatively impact your job performance, don't accept the offer no matter how enticing the pay. There's a better fit out there for you.

Question 6: What is the hiring process?

Find out what the next steps are in the hiring process and when they intend to make a hiring decision. Don't leave without understanding what will happen next and what is expected of you. You need to know whether and when to follow up with your prospective employer so that you are pro-active about the process. As part of this question, I suggest asking why the position is open. By asking this, you may even get more information about company culture and turnover.

Remember, a job interview is a two-way street. Many people go into the interview hoping and praying the company will think they're the right person for the job, but they forget that it's just as important to find out, "Is this job the right one for me?" Better to learn the answer up front. Use the questions suggested and make the most of your interview. With your resume, cover letter, networking skills, and interview abilities in hand, you are ready to go after your dream career with confidence.

Bonus Section #3
Networking Skills for Singles

Networking is one of the most practical tools you can use to advance your career path, and as a single you're never out of place—no partner needed, everyone is welcome. There are many more ways to network these days, and no set rules. Go with your intuition and choose networking tactics that best fit your personality. If you hate to write or talk on the phone, but you really shine in person, then pencil in some networking events on your calendar for upcoming months.

Do you think that online career networking is more your speed and style? Google to find the best networks for your area of expertise. Create great looking profiles for each membership site and start chatting. There are thousands of career-focused networks and resources on the Internet. To locate them online, do a keyword search. You can also look for resources in your local area. Check your hometown newspaper regularly to find out where the best career communities are meeting. Special events are often published in the business section of both weekday and Sunday papers well in advance of meeting dates. When is the next career fair coming to town? When is the next association meeting for your field of interest? If you don't already have one, buy a business appropriate suit or outfit, freshen up your resume, and show up for any career events that spark your interest.

Go out and mingle with like-minded professionals who are seeking a change in their own careers, or who work in the field you would like to pursue. Participate in workshops, contact your college alumni office, or attend networking events. The information is there for the taking; all you have to do is seek it out.

Networking Tips and Guidelines

Networking is still a great way to find a job. Resumes from referrals tend to land on the top of the application pile and are typically reviewed first. You'll want to make the best first impression you can (You can also contact me to find out about "You Had Me at Hello!"—Tips for a 20-second-can't miss-elevator speech). Meanwhile, here are some excellent networking tips for you to use in a group or one-on-one:

1. **Be clear about what you're looking for.** What kind of job or opportunity do you want? Keep your response short and sweet so you can communicate it easily.

2. **Tell everyone you're looking.** This includes friends, family, fellow students, and even professors. You

never know who might know someone in the field you're interested in.

3. **Don't be shy—ask for the referral.** People are usually happy to help and the worst that can happen is that they say no. Remember, nothing ventured, nothing gained.

4. **Follow up.** Send follow-up and thank-you notes to both the potential employers who interviewed you and persons who provided you with the referral.

5. **Find a networking buddy.** If you feel a little shy about reaching out at an event, keep an eye out for someone else new to the game who may appreciate having a networking buddy to lean on. Break the ice with a smile and a general comment on whatever's happening around you. Eventually you can work up to exchanging email addresses and network together during the event, or during future events. Having a support network is a big boost to your confidence, and that can only be good for your career.

6. **Don't overlook opportunities through family and friends.** It may seem a little weird to call up Uncle Ed looking for job leads, but sometimes the best places to find career contacts is through family and friends. The next time a family party or barbecue comes up, use it as a career networking opportu-

nity. You might ask parents or siblings about this ahead of time so you will be better prepared when you meet these people to get them talking about their expertise and ask how they might help you reach your career goals. Most people, especially family members and friends, will be more than willing to lend a hand.

7. **Jump into the conversation.** If you're just getting your feet wet or returning to the networking game after a dry spell, you may feel a little awkward at in-person career events. But like anything, networking gets easier with practice. Everyone at a networking event is there to meet people, so it is okay to jump into a conversation that two or more other people are having. Start by making eye contact and smiling, and then launch your remark and see where it takes you.

8. **Take good care of your career contacts.** The law of attraction states that you get back more of what you put out there. So don't forget to take good care of your new career contacts. If someone does something nice for you, send a handwritten thank-you. If you get great service from, say, the person who does your website, be sure to email them a testimonial. And if you really want to take your networking effort to the next level, volunteer some of your free time. Manage an online forum that relates to

your field. Offer to help with whatever's happening at your local business network.

There are many ways to branch out and meet new people who can become the links in your career networking chain. Once you find some solid contacts, stick by them - they are your lifeblood in the career world. Above all, remember that career networking can be accomplished in many different ways.

9. **Most important—be yourself.** Select the methods that best suit who you are and then give it your all. Soon you'll be sailing on to career networking success. Remember, people connect with people who are real and authentic. You will create stronger contacts if you stay true to yourself and be exactly who you are.

Bonus Section #4
Recommended Career Resources

For additional resources on identifying your ideal career path and making the career transition, visit www.HallieCrawford.com. Here you can find information in my blog and monthly newsletter, as well as numerous career coaching products and services. Customized individual coaching and group coaching sessions are available.

For recommendations on resume writers, headhunters, support for entrepreneurs, and other career transition resources, visit the "Resources" link under "Coaching" on the main menu.

Annotated Bibliography

. . . .

Carson, Rick. *Taming Your Gremlin: A Surprisingly Simple Method for Getting Out of Your Own Way*. New York: Har-perCollins Publishers, 2003.

. . . .

I recommend purchasing *Taming Your Gremlin* to help you manage those negative voices in your head. It is the best how-to guide to teach you strategies for managing those self-defeating thoughts that can hold you back and replacing them with confident ones that spur you on to bigger and better things.

. . . .

Eikleberry, Carol. *The Career Guide for Creative and Unconventional People, 3rd Edition*. Berkley: Ten Speed Press, 2007.

. . . .

This career guide will help you dream outside the box while you are searching for the right career for you. It combines inspirational success stories and self-evaluation tools.

. . . .

Losier, Michael J. *Law of Attraction*. Canada: Michael J. Losier, 2003.

. . . .

Did you like the movie *The Secret?* Read the book *Law of Attraction* by Michael J. Losier to find out how to get what you have always wanted. The book follows a step-by-step process that will help you determine what you really want out of life and how to get it.

. . . .

Tieger, Paul D., and Barron, Barbara. *Do What You Are: Discover the Perfect Career for You Through the Secrets of Personality Type*. New York: Little, Brown Company, 2001.

. . . .

If you think you might be unhappy in your career because your job clashes with your personality, then read: *Do What*

You Are: Discover the Perfect Career for You Through the Secrets of Personality Type. Not only will this book help you avoid careers that you will not enjoy, but it will also help you discover the career that is the best fit for you.

. . . .

Lore, Nicholas. *The Pathfinder, How to Choose or Change Your Career for a Lifetime of Satisfaction and Success.* New York: Simon & Schuster, 1998.

. . . .

This book offers more than 100 self-tests and diagnostic tools to help you choose a new career and provides a step by step process to help you get started on your new path.

About the Author

Hallie Crawford is 100 percent invested in helping clients transform their work lives by guiding them toward their ideal career paths. Her dynamic coaching style is rare: she knows when to be tough, when to be flexible, and she always delivers the kind of encouragement that only true partnership provides. You won't find her sitting on the sidelines cheering you on from afar. Hallie is known for getting out on the field with you. Her secret lies in empowering people to change the way they feel about work. She helps clients see their careers as fulfilling endeavors—extensions of purpose and passion—not just a series of paychecks. You can depend on her to be there for you with empathy and razor-sharp skills.

As clients go through their transitions, it's not unusual for a client to report, "When I bump up against a challenge, I just ask myself, 'What would Hallie say?'" Hallie Crawford is the kind of career coach you too, will want by your side. She knows firsthand the challenges that arise for career seekers in transition. Hallie has developed powerful, practical solutions to make your process smooth and successful. She is passionate about helping others—especially young professionals—because she has taken the same journey in identifying and ultimately achieving her own satisfying career.

Hallie Crawford is a Certified Professional Co-Active Coach (CPCC) with undergraduate and graduate degrees in Communications from Vanderbilt University and the University of Illinois at Chicago. She is a member of the International Coach Federation, Coachville, and serves on the Board of the Georgia Coach Association. She lives in Atlanta with her husband Frank and her son Vaughn.

Blast Off In Your Career Search!

Discover the essential components to a rewarding, fulfilling career. To find out how Hallie can help you identify your ideal career path and make it happen, contact her today to schedule your complimentary consultation: www.HallieCrawford.com or Hallie@HallieCrawford.com.

We'd love to hear from you! Are you ready to share a success story about your career transition? We would love to feature you in our monthly newsletter or blog. Contact Hallie at Hallie@HallieCrawford.com.

Bring Hallie to your next event. Hallie is a compelling, humorous and passionate speaker. Contact us at www.HallieCrawford.com to find out how you can invite her to speak at your next association, club or networking event.

www.HallieCrawford.com
www.FlyingSoloBook.com
www.IKickAssTshirts.com
(404) 228-6434

Bonus Gift for You!

Jumpstart your search for your ideal career with a
50% off coupon for individual coaching with Hallie. Mention
you saw this coupon in *Flying Solo* and you will receive
50% off your 1st month of individual or group coaching.
Hallie would be honored to help you identify your ideal career path!

Printed in the United States
123333LV00002B/184-339/P